I'll Taste Manhattan

I'll Taste Manhattan

PRESENTED BY

THE JUNIOR LEAGUE

OF THE CITY OF

NEW YORK

First Edition
First Printing, April 1994
20,000

Copyright© 1994
The Junior League of the City of New York, Inc.

Library of Congress Number: 94-70312
ISBN: 0-87197-399-3

Manufactured in the United States of America by
Favorite Recipes® Press
2451 Atrium Way
Nashville, Tennessee 37214

All proceeds from the sale of
I'll Taste Manhattan *will benefit the*
charitable activities of the Junior League
of the City of New York.

Additional copies of *I'll Taste Manhattan* may be obtained by writing:
The Junior League of the City of New York, Inc.
Cookbook Committee
130 East 80th Street
New York, NY 10021
212-288-6220

JUNIOR LEAGUE COMMITTEE MEMBERS

Chairmen: ANGELA D. CARABINE • MARY BETH D'AGOSTINO • KATHLEEN L. TYREE

JEAN A. BABENZIEN • MALLORY BLAKE • JANET FUCHS BRUCK • LINDA J. BRUNING • KIMBERLY BURMESTER • SONIA I. CHRISTIAN • KRISTEN COMUZZI • CANDACE CONNORS • CAROLE B. COOKSON • ANNE V. COREY • HELEN E. CUTTING • HEATHER T. DWINELL • ANNE FAIRFAX ELLETT • ANNE M. FERGUSON • LEE FREYER • CHERIE GILLETTE • MAYME GREER • JILL HAMILTON • CATHERINE HENDERSON • SUZANNE EHINGER HENEGHAN • KATHRYN N. HODGES • PATRICIA DAVIS-VON JENA • JULIA JONES • KATHRYN C. KAFFKE • ELIZABETH M. KING • KRISTEN E. KOSSICK • DEE DEE KROPF • ROBIN WILDE LAUCHNOR • CAROLYN C. LAWSON • GEORGINA BLISS MARSHALL • CATHY C. MCCARTHY • JULIE MCNALLY • BETH ANNE MELKMANN • LAURA JENNINGS MEYER • KIMBERLY K. MOORE • SUSAN MULLANEY • ALEXANDRA BLACK NARASIN • MARGOT PEDERSEN • M. BETHANY PINKERTON • NAN POLLOCK • LINDSEY S. PRYOR • BLYTHE RANDOLPH • HEATHER RODTS • ELIZABETH SIGETY • KATHERINE M. SIMON • BARBARA A. TRIESTMAN • LYDIA A. VANDER VOORT • TAMMIS M. VIBBARD • MANDA K. WEINTRAUB • BRETTE E. WESTERLUND • ELIZABETH ZAMOS

SPECIAL ASSISTANCE

New York Junior League Board of Managers:
MELISSA LEWIS BERNSTEIN—PRESIDENT
ELLEN SHICKICH CROMACK—DEVELOPMENT/COMMUNICATIONS VICE PRESIDENT
LUCINDA D. HALE—COMMUNICATIONS MANAGER
COURTENAY A. HARDY—DEVELOPMENT MANAGER
NYJL HEADQUARTERS STAFF

PROFESSIONAL CREDITS

Photography
TOM ECKERLE

Design
JAN MELCHIOR

Food Styling
ELIZABETH KING

Film Processing
COLOR SYSTEMS

Floral Contributions: DAILY BLOSSOM • LARKSPUR
Food Donations: D'AGOSTINO SUPERMARKETS

*The New York Junior League is an
organization of women committed to
promoting volunteerism and to
improving the community through
the effective action and leadership
of trained volunteers.
Its purpose is exclusively educational
and charitable.*

*The New York Junior League
encourages a diverse membership made
up of women who demonstrate
an interest in and commitment to
volunteerism. No woman shall
be excluded from membership
because of race, religion,
national origin or disability.*

CONTENTS

*T*here is little question that the New York hostess ranks among the most innovative and stylish in the world. There are undoubtedly many reasons for this distinction. Two of them provide the theme for this cookbook—an unquenchable desire to express individuality and exposure to a city rich in international influences.

In a city whose sheer mass can assure instant anonymity, it is difficult to stand out and to demonstrate the individuality that is our birthright. In a city whose entire history has been shaped by the consequences of cultural diversity, our personalities cannot help but reflect New York's cultural mosaic. The hallmarks of the New York hostess are flexibility and versatility. Add these attributes to a flair for the unique and a background of diversity and the recipe for successful entertaining—New York-style—is yours to make your own.

I'll Taste Manhattan is full of many tastes and many flavors. The recipes included are as diverse and individual as the neighborhoods, locations and venues that Manhattanites call home. With hundreds of world-class restaurants and daily lives that are uniformly hectic and busy, it is all too easy for New Yorkers to eat out, all the time. *I'll Taste Manhattan* encourages and celebrates the simple but sublime pleasure of entertaining at home.

This book has been designed to please both the novice and the experienced chef alike. Interesting ingredients in some, novel flavor combinations in others, and perhaps just a twist on the traditional in still others—whatever the distinction each recipe will greatly enhance the meal. A menu comprised of simple yet sophisticated dishes may include the introduction of a savory Spiced Butternut Squash Soup followed by an elegant Veal Fontal, Pearl Onion Compote, and Nutted Wild Rice Salad, and end gloriously with a Cranberry Jewel Cake—impressive but not daunting. The more ambitious chef will be challenged by a more complex combination—perhaps featuring a selection of our restaurant recipes starring Bouley's Maine Day-Boat Lobster.

Entertaining should not be a prolonged demonstration of grace under fire. Rather, it should be an expression of friendship, a reflection of yourself, a celebration of sights, sounds and tastes that will linger in the minds of your guests long after the occasion is over. For those who entertain joyfully, with ease and style, great pleasure is sure to be derived from the preparation of many of the recipes included in this book. The more challenging recipes are for entertainment pros who live for the exclamations of a guest's delight. Perhaps you may want to sample several of the dishes sprinkled throughout the book that have been shared by some of New York's most talented chefs. *A Restaurant Sampler*, beginning on page 73, is a collection of recipes from the kitchens of a number of Manhattan's most famous restaurants. Before you take your guests out to dine, try bringing these extraordinary cooking secrets home.

The first chapter of *I'll Taste Manhattan* presents a bountiful array of *Beginnings*—hors d'oeuvre, appetizers, and soups that have been selected for their value as enticements. They are meant to tease the palate with flavors and textures that heighten anticipation for the fare to follow. Dishes with a distinct New York flair such as Beekman Brie and Southstreet Crab Dip are just two of the alluring appetizers that may be found in this chapter. Mousse Royale Phyllo

Triangles and Peppered Citrus Shrimp are both full of flavor, the one rich, the other tangy. For a modern and elegant touch to traditional favorites, try Disheviled Eggs or New-Fashioned Shrimp Cocktail.

A selection of hors d'oeuvre is offered to guests at *Cocktails in a SoHo Loft*, the feature menu compiled for the first chapter on page 16. Thought by many New Yorkers to be the quintessential entertainment, the cocktail party is the perfect opportunity to demonstrate graciousness and style. A successful cocktail party will always leave guests wishing they had been invited to stay for dinner! Whether preparing hors d'oeuvre to accompany drinks or cooking an appetizer to introduce a dinner, remember that a good beginning is the promise of an enchanting evening.

I'll Taste Manhattan's second chapter is devoted to the main event—the entrée that is the centerpiece of the entire meal. Whether casually presented on board a sailboat on the East River,

see *Lunch Under Sail* menu on page 52, or lavishly prepared as a holiday feast for friends and family, see *A Holiday Celebration* menu on page 94, the entrée is the definitive statement of a chef's talent and style. The *Entrées* included in this book

Add ten million cartloads of stone and earth to 843 acres of quarries and swamps, pigsties and shacks, simmer well, and behold—Central Park.

have been selected for their diversity. They reflect the multitude of tastes that characterize Manhattan. In a city of more than 80 native languages, each culture has brought its own cuisine to cast into the melting pot. Whisk well, season to taste, and watch a cuisine peculiar to Manhattan emerge in its many splendored flavors!

The entrées range from a classic Herb-Roasted Chicken to an exotic Pesce Spada all Giudia, from a traditional grilled Butterflied Leg of Lamb to contemporary Venison Medallions. There is sure to be something to surpass the expectations of even the most discerning guests.

Additions comprise the third chapter of *I'll Taste Manhattan*. Like the perfect accessory for a smashing dinner suit, the perfect side dish can make the meal. Often overlooked in favor of an underdone vegetable, a plain potato and a dull green salad, an inspired side dish can transform a meal from the mundane to the magical. A Southern Corn Pudding will add depth of flavor, a Tomato Tart will add a tangy splash of color, a Soufflé au Gruyère will add an elegant richness—each serves to stimulate the palate and enhance the main course offering.

This side dish chapter has been selected to feature two outstanding menu collections—*Tea in the Garden* on page 112, and *Picnic in the Park* on page 134. Set in the elegant garden refuge of New York Junior League Headquarters, tea is served with an accompaniment of delicate sandwiches and a tempting array of dessert confections. For the more casual daytime entertainment, we present a *Picnic in the Park* located on the lush green lawns of New York's incomparable Central Park. Whatever the venue, the breads and muffins, vegetables and potatoes, and salads and sandwiches contained in this chapter will intensify and refresh the mood you have created.

The fourth chapter, *Pastas and Grains*, presents a tantalizing selection of many a New Yorker's favorite foods. Nutritious, endlessly varied, satisfying and simple to prepare, pasta is a universal delight. Enhanced by the flavors of many countries, pasta is one of Italy's most

cherished exports. Pasta can be as light and beguiling as a Fettucini with Poached Lobster or it can be hearty and indulgent like Manicotti with Ratatouille Sauce. It can be as mild as Tagliatelle with Goat Cheese or as hearty as Rigatoni with Porcini and Sau-

Central Park, the 1858 masterpiece of Frederick Law Olmstead's and Calvert Vaux's genius, is still an integral aspect of Manhattan life today.

sage. Pasta's versatility is legendary—it is equally appropriate as a first course, a side dish or even a main course. It can, in fact, be the focus of an entire evening. Consider the *Pasta Kitchen Party*, menu on page 152, for an informal evening of pasta.

The dessert cook will rejoice in the selection of happy *Endings* included in the last chapter of *I'll Taste Manhattan*. Dessert is the crowning achievement of any hostess' reign and is your guests' final impression of your entertainment style and culinary skills. Whether you choose the decadent richness of Dripping Springs Pecan Pie or the more restrained and refined Light Apricot Soufflé, your guests will leave with the memory of a dazzling dessert. Indulge them in the sin of a Chocolate Pâté or enchant them with the tangy freshness of a Lemon Tart—any choice in this chapter will bring accolades.

If the choice is too difficult or if you want to sustain the gaiety and glamour of New York at night, why not host a *Midnight Dessert Buffet*? The array of sweets and confections on this sample menu on page 188 is presented in the elegant and intimate Fifth Avenue setting of the National

Academy of Design—a city oasis of serenity and beauty. Since even good things must come to an end, conclude your evening with one or more of the many delectable desserts. They will make for sweet goodbyes.

The over 2,300 trained women volunteers who are members of the New York Junior League hope you will enjoy entertaining with this cookbook. It is the first cookbook that the New York Junior League has published in two decades. Now, as then, all proceeds from the sale of *I'll Taste Manhattan* will benefit the charitable activities of the New York Junior League.

By purchasing this book, you join corporations, foundations, and other individuals in financing New York Junior League programs which reach, among others, homeless families, disadvantaged minority youths, the isolated elderly, and terminally-ill children. New York Junior League members volunteer in police precinct houses, museums, and hospitals; they advocate on

Hansom carriage rides in Manhattan have been a tradition for generations. Here, a historical glimpse of the Plaza Hotel.

behalf of women and children, and teach life skills to imprisoned women offenders—just several examples of the work in which we are involved. The depth and breadth of our commitment is demonstrated by the over 150,000 hours of community service we donate each year.

Founded in 1901, the New York Junior League was the first of the 284 Junior Leagues that now exist in the United States, Canada, Mexico and England. For over 90 years, the New York Junior League has been a force for positive change in the community. Our tradition of service continues today with the publication of *I'll Taste Manhattan.*

BEGINNINGS

APPETIZERS
SOUPS
BEVERAGES

$\mathcal{B}$eginnings—the first taste of flavors to come .... Whether kindling a new romance, embarking on a new career, or sampling a new menu, beginnings are a time for celebration, a time to create lasting impressions and a time when anticipation and expectations run high.

Hors d'oeuvre, appetizers, and soups all set the stage for the flavors, colors, and textures to follow. They define not only the style and substance of the rest of the meal, but of the chef as well. Whether the occasion calls for the formal sophistication of Cold Curried Avocado Soup, the elegant simplicity of Salmon Pâté, or the casual richness of Cheddar Cheese Shortbreads, the recipes in this first chapter of *I'll Taste Manhattan* will create the perfect impression and surpass the expectations of even the most discerning guests.

The ideal beginning of many a successful Manhattan evening is the ubiquitous cocktail party. Traditionally hosted as a festive prelude to dinner, the cocktail party has come to represent the ultimate Manhattan entertainment for many New Yorkers. Few Manhattanites admit to having any free time at all and even fewer are content with the size of their apartment kitchens—for these reasons, the cocktail party is one of the most frequently hosted evening entertainments, requiring modest commitments of both time and space. As elegant and formal as champagne and caviar or as casual and down-home as beer and tapas, the cocktail party's parameters are restricted only by the imagination and taste of the cook who creates it.

How better to illustrate the evolution of pre-dinner drinks into a nearly all-inclusive dining experience, than by presenting *Cocktails in a SoHo Loft*? Taking its name from the street location where it begins ("South of Houston"), SoHo was once a bastion of the artistic off-beat. Today, SoHo is a unique blend of diverse styles, cultures and tastes—as diverse, in fact, as the hors d'oeuvre listed on this chapter's cocktail party menu. From Asparagus Spears with Lemon Parmesan Dipping Sauce to Sweet Mustard Shrimp, from Polenta with Dilled Goat Cheese to Mousse Royale Canapes—these and other delectable choices provide the foundation for fabulous entertaining.

MENU
Cocktails in a SoHo Loft

ASPARAGUS SPEARS WITH LEMON
PARMESAN DIPPING SAUCE

BABY POTATO PANCAKES WITH
CREME FRAICHE AND CAVIAR

MOUSSE ROYALE CANAPES

SWEET MUSTARD SHRIMP

WARM PEPPERED FILET OF BEEF WITH
HORSERADISH CREAM

SALMON TARTARE ON TOASTED BRIOCHE

ENDIVE SPEARS WITH
SOUTHSTREET CRAB DIP

CURRIED CHICKEN TARTLETS

POLENTA WITH DILLED GOAT CHEESE

SELECTION OF SPIRITS FOR
CLASSIC COCKTAILS

Left overleaf, *iced vodka compliments Baby Potato Pancakes with crème fraîche and caviar.*

Left above, *antique sterling silver cocktail plates display an enticing selection of hors d'oeuvre.*

Below far left, *pink hydrangea offset a service plate of skewered Sweet Mustard Shrimp.*

Below near left, *Salmon Tartare on squares of toasted brioche.*

At right, *pumpernickel starlets piped with Mousse Royale Pâté. A delicious apple accompanies sweet cornichon pickles and olives.*

Right overleaf, *piano music provides the focal point for cocktails.*

Far right overleaf top to bottom, *Curried Chicken Tartlets, Polenta with Dilled Goat Cheese, thin slices of Warm Peppered Fillet of Beef with Horseradish Cream.*

POLENTA WITH DILLED GOAT CHEESE

Serves Twelve

O*ne could think of polenta as Italian cornmeal. Look for "instant polenta" to save time.*

Mash the goat cheese with a fork in a bowl. Add the dill, 1 tablespoon olive oil, wine, and half the tomatoes; mix well.

Fry the polenta slices in additional olive oil in a sauté pan until light brown; drain on a paper towel.

Spread the cheese mixture on the polenta slices; top with the remaining tomatoes. Serve on individual serving plates.

Note To prepare polenta slices, spread prepared polenta in a 10-by-15-inch pan. Let stand until cool. Cut into 3-inch squares or into decorative shapes with a cookie or biscuit cutter.

3–4 ounces goat cheese

1 tablespoon chopped fresh dill

1 tablespoon olive oil

1 tablespoon dry white wine

7 sundried tomatoes in oil, chopped

slices of firm polenta

olive oil for frying

MINI PAN BAGNAS

Serves Thirty-Six to Forty-Two

F*rom The Party Box caterer, this recipe can go two ways: as an hors d'oeuvre or as picnic fare.*

Slice almost through the baguette lengthwise, leaving one side intact. Scoop out the soft bread. Sprinkle the inside of the remaining shell with the vinaigrette.

Drain and chop the artichoke hearts. Layer the salami, pepperoni, cheese, peppers, lettuce, artichokes, tomatoes, and onion in the baguette, sprinkling with additional vinaigrette. Wrap the stuffed bread tightly with plastic wrap. Place between two cutting boards. Chill, weighted, overnight.

Slice the baguette on an angle into ¼- to ½-inch slices to serve; arrange on a serving plate.

Variation For cocktail parties, choose a very thin baguette. For picnic fare, select a heartier baguette, as is shown on page 133.

1 24-inch onion sourdough baguette

⅓ cup Italian-style vinaigrette

1 7-ounce jar marinated artichoke hearts

4 ounces each salami and pepperoni, thinly sliced

4 ounces provolone cheese, thinly sliced

1 2-ounce jar roasted red peppers, chopped

½ cup chopped romaine lettuce

1 or 2 plum tomatoes, thinly sliced

½ cup chopped red onion

BEEKMAN BRIE

A great hors d'oeuvre that is sophisticated, but easy. It is perfect with French bread or water biscuits.

1/4 cup apricot preserves

1 2-pound wheel of brie cheese

8 ounces frozen phyllo dough, thawed

1/2 cup melted unsalted butter

fresh dill

red and green grapes

green apple wedges

pear wedges

Spread the preserves on the top of the cheese. Layer the thawed phyllo dough on a work surface, brushing each sheet with the melted butter; keep the unused portions of the dough covered with a damp cloth to keep the sheets from drying out as you work.

Place the cheese on the phyllo layers; fold the pastry around the cheese, enclosing the cheese completely. Brush with the remaining butter. Chill, covered, in the refrigerator.

Preheat the oven to 425° F. Place the phyllo-wrapped brie in a shallow baking pan. Bake for about 10 minutes or until the pastry is golden brown. Let stand for 10 minutes. Place on a serving plate. Garnish with the dill, grapes, apple wedges, and pear wedges.

Note The term hors d'oeuvre literally translated means "outside the work (meal)." Regardless of how many hors d'oeuvre you serve, it is always spelled "hors d'oeuvre," because it is referring to the singular work.

DISHEVILED EGGS

T his is an attractive and tasty way to serve traditional deviled eggs.

12 extra-large eggs, hard-boiled

1/4 cup unsalted butter, softened

2 tablespoons Dijon mustard

1/2 cup mayonnaise

salt and freshly ground pepper to taste

chopped fresh flat parsley

Cut the eggs into halves lengthwise. Remove the yolks to a food processor; process until smooth. Add the butter, mustard, mayonnaise, salt, and pepper; process again until smooth.

Stuff the egg yolk mixture into the egg whites with a spoon or pastry bag. Press the halves together gently. Garnish with the parsley. Chill until serving time.

CHEDDAR CHEESE SHORTBREADS

Serves Twenty

Served with a nice full-bodied red wine, this simple appetizer makes a delightful light hors d'oeuvre.

Preheat the oven to 350° F.

Combine the butter, flour, cheese, salt, red pepper, and pecans in a bowl; mix well. Shape the dough into 1-inch balls.

Place the balls on a baking sheet; press with a fork to flatten. Bake for 12 minutes. Remove to brown paper on a wire rack to cool.

Note These shortbreads freeze well.

Variation Substitute cracked black pepper for the red pepper and Swiss cheese for the cheddar cheese to vary these shortbreads.

- 3/4 cup plus 2 tablespoons unsalted butter, softened
- 2 1/2 cups flour
- 2 cups shredded sharp cheddar cheese
- 1 teaspoon salt
- 1/4–1/2 teaspoon red pepper
- 1 cup chopped pecans or walnuts

PROVENÇAL TORTE

Serves Twelve

Especially pretty if the mold is lined with a design of basil leaves or edible flowers which will show when it is inverted for serving. Great for brunch.

Line a 5-by-9-inch pan, bowl, or mold with plastic wrap. Combine the cream cheese, goat cheese, and butter in a bowl; beat until smooth. Line the bottom and sides of the prepared pan, bowl, or mold with the sliced cheese, reserving several slices for the top. Layer the pesto, tomatoes, pine nuts, and cheese mixture 1/3 at a time in the pan. Top with the reserved cheese slices.

Place a layer of damp cheesecloth over the torte; cover with plastic wrap. Add a second weighted pan or mold to press the torte down. Chill overnight or for up to 4 days.

Remove the top plastic wrap and cheesecloth from the torte and invert it onto a serving plate; remove the remaining plastic wrap. Serve with the crackers or toast points.

- 8 ounces cream cheese, softened
- 2–3 ounces goat cheese, softened
- 1/2 cup unsalted butter, softened
- 8 ounces provolone or Italian fontina cheese, sliced
- 1/2 cup (or more) drained good-quality pesto
- 4 ounces sundried tomatoes, chopped
- 1/4–1/3 cup chopped pine nuts or walnuts, lightly toasted
- firm crackers or toast points

ROQUEFORT AND ONION TARTLETS

B*ite-sized tarts are a substantial addition to any cocktail party.*

For the pastry

1/2 cup unsalted butter
1 cup flour
   pinch of salt
3 tablespoons water

For the filling

4 large onions
2 tablespoons unsalted butter
   thyme, salt, and pepper to taste
7 ounces Roquefort cheese, crumbled
1 egg
2 egg yolks
1/4 cup milk
3/4 cup cream
   nutmeg to taste

Dean & DeLuca, at 560 Broadway, is a Manhattan tradition in fine food. Their wide range of sumptuous desserts and esoteric produce is particularly noteworthy.

TO MAKE THE PASTRY:

Preheat the oven to 400° F.

Cut the butter into a mixture of flour and salt in a bowl until the mixture resembles coarse crumbs. Add the water a small amount at a time, mixing to form a soft dough that leaves the side of the bowl clean.

Roll the dough thin on a floured surface. Cut the dough into circles slightly larger than the tartlet cups. Fit the circles into the cups and trim the edges; prick the bottoms with a fork. Bake for 7 to 8 minutes or until partially cooked.

TO MAKE THE FILLING AND BAKE:

Cut the onions into thin slices. Combine the slices with the thyme, salt, and pepper in a heavy saucepan. Cover with a piece of buttered foil, pressing down gently; cover.

Cook over low heat for 20 to 30 minutes or until the onions are very tender but not brown. Stir in the cheese with a wooden spoon. Cool slightly. Spoon the onion mixture into the partially-baked shells.

Beat the egg and egg yolks with the milk, cream, nutmeg, salt, and pepper in a bowl. Spoon over the onions in the tartlet shells, filling the shells 3/4 full. Bake the tartlets for several minutes or until the custard is partially set. Add enough remaining custard to fill the shells. Bake for 10 to 15 minutes longer or until the custard is puffed and brown. Serve hot or cooled.

Note These tartlets can be made one day in advance, but the pastry tends to become soggy if it stands too long. Keep the tartlets tightly covered in the refrigerator and reheat at 350° F. just until warm; do not overheat.

Variation The pastry tartlets may also be filled with any of the savory salads in this book or with Fresh Tuna Tartare (see page 35).

CHICKEN ENCHILADA PINWHEELS

Serves Eight

Take any party south of the border with this unusual appetizer which may be made several days in advance.

2 whole chicken breasts

1/2 4-ounce can chopped green chili peppers

1 4-ounce can chopped black olives

1 4-ounce can stuffed green olives, chopped

1 bunch scallions with some green tops, chopped

16 ounces cream cheese, softened

1 1/2 cups shredded sharp cheddar cheese

1 package 10-inch flour tortillas

Rinse the chicken and pat dry. Poach in water to cover in a saucepan until tender; drain. Chop the chicken into small pieces, discarding the skin and bones.

Combine the green chili peppers, olives, scallions, and cheeses in a bowl. Add the chicken; mix well. Spread the mixture in a thin layer on the tortillas. Roll the tortillas to enclose the filling. Arrange in a single layer on a plate. Cover with a slightly moistened paper towel; wrap well with plastic wrap. Chill for up to 3 days.

Cut the tortilla rolls into 1/4-inch slices. Serve the pinwheels as an appetizer or with any traditional Mexican accompaniment, such as guacamole, sour cream, or a salsa dip.

SKEWERED GINGER CHICKEN

Serves Six to Eight

A wonderful hors d'oeuvre for your next cocktail party.

3–4 boneless chicken breasts

2 tablespoons soy sauce

1 teaspoon grated fresh ginger root

1 teaspoon crushed garlic

3 tablespoons cornstarch

1 tablespoon sesame oil

6 tablespoons vegetable oil

1 bunch scallions, sliced

Rinse chicken breasts and pat dry; cut into bite-sized pieces.

Combine the soy sauce, ginger, garlic, and cornstarch in a bowl; mix until smooth. Add the chicken; mix to coat well.

Heat the sesame oil and vegetable oil in a wok or heavy cast-iron skillet. Add the chicken. Cook until golden brown; drain well. Serve on bamboo skewers with hot Chinese mustard. Garnish with scallions.

Variation Delicious with rice as an entrée.

DILLED CUCUMBER MOUSSE

Serves Six to Eight

Very simple, tasty and refreshing, this mousse is especially good in the summer when cucumbers are abundant.

Soften the gelatin in the cold water in a bowl. Add the boiling water; mix well. Process in a food processor until the gelatin dissolves. Add the mayonnaise, scallions, lemon juice, dill, and red pepper sauce; mix well. Stir in the cucumbers.

Spoon the mixture into a small mold. Chill for 4 hours or overnight. Dip the mold in hot water. Unmold onto a radicchio-lined serving plate.

2 envelopes unflavored gelatin

1/4 cup cold water

1/2 cup boiling water

1 cup mayonnaise

1 tablespoon sliced scallions

1 tablespoon fresh lemon juice

1/2 teaspoon dill

dash of red pepper sauce

2 medium cucumbers, peeled, seeded, chopped

radicchio

SOUTHSTREET CRAB DIP

Serves Twelve

Wonderful on endive spears, cucumber slices, or piped into cherry tomatoes.

Preheat the oven to 350° F.

Combine the cream cheese, crab meat, onion, pepper, sour cream, sherry, and red pepper sauce in a bowl; mix well. Spoon the mixture into a 2-cup baking dish.

Bake for about 15 minutes or until hot and bubbly. Serve hot with the crackers, toast points, or bagel chips.

8 ounces cream cheese, softened

6–8 ounces crab meat, shredded

2 tablespoons finely chopped fresh onion or dried onion flakes

1/4 teaspoon seasoned pepper

1/2 cup sour cream

1 tablespoon sherry

dash of red pepper sauce

SPINACH DIP

This has been a long-time favorite at the New York Junior League headquarters.

½ cup parsley leaves

3 tablespoons fresh dill

1 teaspoon fresh oregano

1 teaspoon fresh chervil

1 teaspoon fresh basil

2 10-ounce packages frozen spinach, thawed, drained

1 bunch scallions

1 large white onion

2 cups mayonnaise

8 ounces cream cheese, softened

3 tablespoons fresh lemon juice

4 ounces country Dijon mustard

salt and freshly ground pepper to taste

Wash the fresh herbs and blot or spin dry. Combine the herbs with the spinach, scallions, onion, mayonnaise, cream cheese, lemon juice, mustard, salt, and pepper in a food processor container.

Process until all the ingredients are smooth and well blended. Chill, covered, for 6 hours or for up to 1 week.

Serve with crudités or chips.

Note To get the most juice out of lemons, roll the lemons on a table before squeezing.

Variation Use leftover dip in place of mayonnaise on any favorite sandwiches.

TRICOLORED DIPPING SAUCES

Dipping sauces are great as dips for crudités or for use as sandwich spreads. Try the Quick Basil Dipping Sauce on a grilled chicken sandwich, or the Roasted Red Pepper Dipping Sauce on fresh mozzarella cheese.

TO MAKE THE ROASTED RED PEPPER DIPPING SAUCE:

Process the red peppers in a food processor until the peppers are finely minced. Add the tomato paste, egg, and egg yolk; process until the mixture is smooth. Add the oil gradually, processing constantly and scraping the bowl occasionally. Add the lemon juice, salt, and white pepper; mix well.

TO MAKE THE QUICK BASIL DIPPING SAUCE:

Combine the garlic with the egg, lemon juice, basil, and salt in a food processor container; process until the mixture is smooth. Add the oils gradually, processing constantly until smooth. Season with additional salt and pepper.

TO MAKE THE LEMON PARMESAN DIPPING SAUCE:

Combine the egg yolk, lemon juice, salt, and pepper in a food processor container or a bowl; process or beat until smooth. Add the olive oil in a steady stream, mixing constantly until thickened. Stir in the lemon zest and Parmesan cheese. Adjust the seasonings.

Note Serve each dipping sauce in an individual bowl. A tablespoon or more of boiling water added to a finished dipping sauce will help to keep it from separating.

Variation Add Dijon mustard or finely chopped red shallot to the Lemon Parmesan Dipping Sauce. For Remoulade Sauce, add small amounts of anchovy paste, chopped gherkins, capers, parsley, and tarragon.

Roasted Red Pepper Dipping Sauce

1½ 4-ounce jars roasted red peppers, drained, patted dry

1 tablespoon tomato paste

1 egg, at room temperature

1 egg yolk

1½ cups olive oil, or 3/4 cup each vegetable oil and olive oil

lemon juice, salt, and white pepper to taste

Quick Basil Dipping Sauce

1 clove of garlic, mashed

1 large egg

4 teaspoons fresh lemon juice

2 cups loosely packed washed basil leaves

1/2 teaspoon salt

3/4 cup vegetable oil

1/4 cup olive oil

Lemon Parmesan Dipping Sauce

1 egg yolk, at room temperature

4 tablespoons fresh lemon juice

salt and freshly ground pepper to taste

1 cup olive oil

grated zest of 2 lemons

1/2 cup grated Parmesan cheese

ZUCCHINI BISCUITS

Serves Forty-Eight

Dress up a cocktail party by cutting these into fancy shapes with a cookie cutter or diagonally into diamonds.

3 cups grated zucchini

1 cup Bisquick baking mix

1½ cups chopped onion

½ cup grated Parmesan cheese

2 tablespoons chopped parsley

salt, seasoned salt, oregano and freshly ground pepper to taste

1 clove of garlic, chopped

½ cup vegetable oil

4 eggs

Preheat the oven to 350° F. Combine the zucchini, baking mix, onion, Parmesan cheese, parsley, salt, seasoned salt, oregano, pepper, garlic, oil, and eggs in a large bowl; mix well.

Spoon the mixture into a 9-by-13-inch baking pan. Bake for 25 minutes or until set and golden brown. Cut into squares. Serve warm.

Note These appetizers may be made ahead and frozen.

Variation Split the biscuits and add proscuitto and roasted red pepper for tasty cocktail sandwiches.

SAUTEED FOIE GRAS

F*rom Tavern on the Green restaurant—a New York institution nestled in the heart of Central Park. Lady apples and fried polenta crescents add a wonderful dimension to this traditional favorite.*

For the polenta crescents

1 cup polenta mix
salt to taste
4 cups boiling water

For the sauce

3 tablespoons chopped shallots
1 tablespoon clarified unsalted butter
1/4 teaspoon cumin
1/4 teaspoon coriander
1 2-inch cinnamon stick
1/2 cup Calvados
2 cups veal stock

For the presentation

8 slices *foie gras*
2 tablespoons unsalted butter
12 lady apples, peeled, cut into quarters
2 tablespoons grated lemon zest

TO MAKE THE POLENTA CRESCENTS:
Cook the polenta with the salt in the boiling water in a saucepan until thick. Spread in a shallow pan. Let stand until cool. Cut into crescents with a cutter.

TO MAKE THE SAUCE:
Sauté the shallots in the clarified butter in a saucepan until tender. Add the cumin, coriander, and cinnamon stick. Cook until the mixture begins to caramelize. Add the Calvados, stirring to deglaze the saucepan.
Stir in the veal stock. Cook until the mixture is reduced by half. Correct the seasoning. Keep the sauce warm. Remove the cinnamon stick from the sauce.

TO MAKE THE APPETIZER:
Cook the polenta crescents on a greased griddle until lightly browned on both sides; keep the crescents warm.
Sauté the *foie gras* a few slices at a time in the 2 tablespoons unsalted butter in a sauté pan. Remove the *foie gras* to a heated platter.
Sauté the apples lightly in the sauté pan; remove to a warm plate. Sauté the lemon zest lightly in the sauté pan.
Arrange the *foie gras* slices and polenta crescents on four individual serving plates. Arrange the apples around them. Spoon the sauce over the top; sprinkle with the lemon zest. Serve immediately.

Far left overleaf, SoHo, a former industrial district bordered by Sixth Avenue and Lafayette, Houston and Canal Streets, now has a wide variety of furnishing and antique shops, contemporary art galleries, and unique boutiques.

Near left overleaf, the elaborate cornice of the Mercer Arms is typical of the architectural detail that can be enjoyed by the observant pedestrian on a stroll around SoHo.

MOUSSE ROYALE PHYLLO TRIANGLES

Serves Sixty

From *Les Trois Petite Cochons, New York's source for pâté.*

Preheat the oven to 350° F. Melt the 2 tablespoons butter in a medium saucepan. Heat the butter until it begins to bubble. Add the mushrooms. Cook until the liquid has evaporated.

Add the cognac. Cook until the cognac is completely reduced. Cool to room temperature. Combine the mousse, chives, and pistachios in a bowl. Add the mushroom mixture; mix well. Season with the salt and pepper.

Place 1 sheet of the phyllo dough at a time on the work surface. Brush the sheets with a mixture of the clarified butter and olive oil. Cut the sheets into 2½-inch squares.

Place 1 tablespoon of the filling on one corner of each square. Fold the dough to form triangles and fold again to form smaller triangles. Place the triangles on a baking sheet. Bake for 10 to 12 minutes or until light brown.

Variation Put prepared mousse pâté into a pastry bag fitted with a ½-inch star tip and pipe onto cocktail bread that has been cut into decorative shapes. Garnish with olives and cornichons, as is shown on page 19.

2 tablespoons unsalted butter

1 cup finely minced cremini mushrooms

2 tablespoons cognac

4 pounds goose liver mousse

2 tablespoons minced chives

1 cup minced pistachios

salt and freshly ground pepper to taste

3–4 packages Apollo phyllo pastry

1 pound unsalted butter, clarified

⅔ cup olive oil

BABY POTATO PANCAKES

Serve with crème fraîche and caviar for an extra special touch.

1 pound russet potatoes, finely grated

1 tablespoon finely chopped onion

3 egg yolks, slightly beaten

salt and freshly ground pepper to taste

½ cup vegetable oil

Place the potatoes on a kitchen towel. Squeeze the potatoes in the towel to remove as much moisture as possible.

Combine the potatoes with the onion, egg yolks, salt, and pepper in a bowl; mix well.

Heat the oil in a large sauté pan. Drop the potato mixture by tablespoonfuls into the oil, pressing into thin cakes. Fry for 8 to 10 minutes or until golden brown on both sides. Serve warm.

SMOKED SALMON BRUSCHETTA

Bruschetta, an Italian open-faced appetizer, may also be served with the toppings of your choice.

3 tablespoons pine nuts

2 medium tomatoes, seeded, finely chopped

4 ounces mozzarella cheese, finely chopped

4 ounces smoked salmon, finely chopped

3 tablespoons olive oil

salt and white pepper to taste

4 large slices French country bread

1 clove of garlic, cut into halves

8 basil leaves, cut into thin strips

Toast the pine nuts in a small sauté pan over medium-high heat until golden brown. Cool to room temperature.

Preheat the broiler.

Combine the toasted pine nuts with the tomatoes, cheese, salmon, and olive oil in a bowl. Add the salt and pepper; mix well.

Arrange the bread slices on a baking sheet. Toast in the broiler until golden brown on both sides. Rub the cut side of the garlic on one side of each bread slice. Spoon the tomato mixture onto the bread. Arrange on a serving plate; garnish with the basil strips. Serve immediately.

NORWEGIAN GRAVLAX

Serves Twenty

Gravlax is delicious served on thinly sliced French bread or toast points. Accompany with sweetened mustard and cornichon pickles or dill sprigs. Few appetizers are more elegant.

Rinse the salmon and pat dry. Place the skin side down in a rectangular glass dish. Sprinkle with the salt and sugar. Pour the vermouth and brandy down the side of the dish; top with the juniper berries, bay leaves, and dill. Cover with plastic wrap and weight slightly.

Cure in the refrigerator for 3 to 5 days; drain, reserving the curing liquid to use again if desired.

Slice the salmon very thin on the diagonal from the top side to the skin side. Arrange on a serving plate.

Note This is an excellent choice for large entertaining because it must be prepared in advance.

2 pounds salmon fillets
1/3 cup kosher salt
3/4 cup sugar
1/2 cup white vermouth
1/2 cup brandy
3/4 cup juniper berries
2 bay leaves
1 large bunch dill

FRESH TUNA TARTARE

Serves Ten

An updated version of a delicious classic. Serve on toasted and lightly buttered sliced brioche.

Process the tuna to the consistency of ground beef in a food processor; do not overprocess. Combine with the olive oil, dill, shallots, lemon juice, salt, and pepper in a bowl; mix lightly.

Spoon into a serving bowl; arrange the toast points or black bread around the tuna. Sprinkle with the black sesame seeds if desired.

Variation May substitute fresh salmon for fresh tuna.

1 pound center-cut tuna steak
1/4 cup extra-virgin olive oil
1/4 cup chopped fresh dill
1/3 cup finely chopped shallots
fresh lemon juice to taste
salt and freshly ground pepper to taste
toast points or black bread
black sesame seeds (optional)

SALMON PATE

Select a beautiful mold for a touch of elegance before dinner.

10 ounces salmon, poached
3 ounces smoked salmon
4 ounces cream cheese, softened
1 tablespoon mayonnaise
1 tablespoon grated onion
1 tablespoon fresh lemon juice
1/8 teaspoon white pepper
1 tablespoon red pepper sauce
1 tablespoon horseradish
   sour cream, fresh dill

Combine the salmon, cream cheese, mayonnaise, onion, lemon juice, white pepper, red pepper sauce, and horseradish in a bowl; mix well.

Spoon into a 5-by-7-inch loaf pan or a mold. Chill until firm. Unmold the pâté onto a serving plate. Frost with the sour cream; garnish with the dill.

Note Great served with pumpernickel or rye cocktail bread.

NEW-FASHIONED SHRIMP COCKTAIL

Serves Six

Martini *glasses make the presentation of this recipe from the restaurant Arcadia spectacular.*

Marinate the peeled shrimp in lemon juice and olive oil for 2 hours. Combine the remaining ingredients except the red leaf lettuce. Drain the shrimp and add to the vegetable and fruit mixture.

Fill martini glasses with the shredded lettuce. Mound the shrimp cocktail on each lettuce nest.

Note Large or jumbo shrimp can be substituted for the Santa Barbara shrimp.

The wrought-iron lamps at left are examples of the objets d'art available from purveyors of home furnishings in SoHo.

12 ounces Santa Barbara shrimp, peeled
1/2 cup fresh lemon juice
1/2 cup olive oil
1 cup chopped tomato
1/2 cup chopped red bell pepper
1/2 cup corn kernels
1/2 cup finely chopped red onion
1/4 cup chopped chives
1/2 cup chopped fresh parsley
1/2 cup finely chopped carrot
1 cup grapefruit juice
grated zest of 2 grapefruit
1 avocado, finely chopped
1 papaya, finely chopped
pinch of cayenne pepper
salt and freshly ground black pepper to taste
1 head red leaf lettuce, finely shredded

Serves Six

From the renowned Le Cirque restaurant, this is a lovely dish with a beautiful presentation.

For the sauce

6 shallots, sliced

2 cups white wine

1 tablespoon unsalted butter

1 sprig of chervil

1 cup heavy cream, whipped

For the chartreuse

24 medium shrimp

1 cup olive oil

3 eggplant

4 zucchini

6 large ripe tomatoes, peeled, seeded

Left overleaf, more of the varied treasures that abound in SoHo shops.

TO MAKE THE SAUCE:

Combine the shallots with the wine in a 10-inch saucepan. Cook until the liquid has nearly evaporated. Add the butter and chervil; mix well and set aside. Add the whipped cream at serving time; mix gently.

TO MAKE THE CHARTREUSE:

Sauté the shrimp lightly in a small amount of the olive oil in a sauté pan. Shrimp should remain uncooked.

Slice the eggplant ¼ inch thick and the zucchini ⅛ inch thick. Sauté separately in some of the remaining olive oil in a sauté pan. Drain on a paper towel.

Sauté the tomatoes in the remaining olive oil in a sauté pan; drain. Crush the tomatoes with a fork to form a coarse purée.

Place 1 slice of the eggplant in the bottom of individual 3-inch tin molds. Arrange 4 shrimp in a *rosace* (pinwheel) pattern on the eggplant in each mold. Spread with a small amount of the tomato purée. Arrange the zucchini slices on top.

Place the molds in a *bain marie* (water bath) in a saucepan. Cook for 10 minutes. Drain for 2 minutes.

Remove to a serving plate. Spoon the sauce over the top.

PEPPERED CITRUS SHRIMP

Serves Ten

May be prepared with chicken instead of shrimp or served over mesclun or baby greens as a warm salad.

Rinse and drain the shrimp. Combine with the lemon juice, olive oil, black pepper, garlic, cayenne pepper, and paprika in a large bowl; mix well. Marinate, covered, at room temperature for 2 hours or in the refrigerator for up to 8 hours, tossing occasionally. Drain, reserving the marinade.

Preheat the grill.

Grill the shrimp for 5 to 10 minutes or until cooked through, turning and basting frequently with the reserved marinade. Serve on skewers warm or at room temperature; garnish with the lemon and/or lime wedges.

2 pounds extra-large unpeeled shrimp, deveined

1/2 cup fresh lemon juice and/or lime juice

1/2 cup olive oil

2 tablespoons coarsely ground black pepper

2 large cloves of garlic, minced

cayenne pepper to taste

1/2 teaspoon paprika

lemon and/or lime wedges

SWEET MUSTARD SHRIMP

Serves Ten to Twelve

An elegant first course that can be prepared in advance.

Combine the Dijon mustard, dry mustard, mustard seeds, lemon juice, sugar, and cider vinegar in a bowl. Whisk in the oil. Stir in the cinnamon, dill, and onion. Chill, tightly covered, for up to one week.

Steam the shrimp; peel and devein. Add to the marinade. Marinate in the refrigerator for 2 hours to overnight. Serve over a bed of greens.

Variation Serve shrimp on wooden skewers as a wonderful hors d'oeuvre, as shown on page 18.

1/2 cup Dijon mustard

2 teaspoons dry mustard

1 teaspoon toasted mustard seeds

1–2 tablespoons fresh lemon juice

6 tablespoons sugar

1/4 cup cider vinegar

1/2 cup vegetable oil

1 teaspoon cinnamon

2 tablespoons dill

2 tablespoons finely chopped red onion

2 pounds medium shrimp

CARROT AND YELLOW PEPPER SOUP

D*elicious with Park Picnic Cheese-Herb Bread.*

3 tablespoons unsalted butter

3 large carrots, peeled

1 large yellow bell pepper

1 cup sliced leeks

3 sprigs of fresh rosemary

ground cumin to taste

3½ cups homemade chicken stock

salt and freshly ground pepper to taste

Melt the butter in a saucepan over medium heat. Cut the carrots into ¼-inch slices and yellow pepper into 1-inch squares. Add the carrots, leeks, bell pepper, rosemary, and cumin; mix well. Cook, covered, over medium heat for 10 minutes, stirring occasionally.

Add the chicken stock, salt, and pepper; mix well. Simmer, uncovered, for 20 minutes or until the carrots are tender. Discard the rosemary sprigs.

Process the mixture in a food processor or blender until smooth; adjust the seasonings. Ladle into soup bowls. Serve soup hot with warmed bread.

SPINACH YOGURT SOUP

A *light and easy favorite that can be garnished with lemon rounds for a festive touch.*

10 ounces fresh spinach

1 large onion, coarsely chopped

1 cup water

2 cups plain yogurt

¾ cup chicken broth

Rinse the spinach; drain. Remove the stems and tough center veins in the larger leaves.

Combine the spinach, onion, and water in a stockpot. Cook for 5 minutes or until the spinach is wilted and the onion is tender; drain. Purée the mixture in a food processor. Add the yogurt. Process until blended.

Return the spinach mixture to the stockpot. Stir in the chicken broth. Cook until heated through, stirring constantly. Ladle into soup bowls.

Note May store in the refrigerator for one to two days. An excellent addition to a "make-ahead" picnic.

IROQUOIS CORN CHOWDER

Serves Six to Eight

Add a jalapeño pepper for a south-of-the border accent to this native American dish.

Fry the bacon in a saucepan until crisp; drain and crumble, reserving 1 tablespoon of the drippings. Combine the reserved drippings and butter in a sauté pan. Add the onions; sauté until tender, stirring constantly.

Stir in the flour. Cook until light brown, stirring constantly. Add the chicken stock, potatoes, corn, bell peppers, green chilies, scallions, jalapeño pepper, and cilantro. Cook over low heat for 20 to 30 minutes or until the potatoes are tender, stirring occasionally.

Add additional stock or water if the soup is too thick. Season with the salt and pepper. Ladle into soup bowls. Sprinkle the bacon over the soup. Serve immediately.

4 ounces bacon

2 tablespoons unsalted butter

2 cups chopped onions

2 tablespoons unbleached flour

4 cups chicken stock

2 large potatoes, peeled, chopped

2 10-ounce packages frozen corn, cooked, drained

1 red bell pepper, chopped

1 green bell pepper, chopped

1 4-ounce can green chilies, drained, chopped

3 scallions, minced

1 jalapeño pepper, seeded, finely chopped (optional)

1–2 tablespoons chopped cilantro

salt and freshly ground pepper to taste

CAJUN CRAB GUMBO

You *need not to go to New Orleans to savor this Cajun specialty.*

For the gumbo

- 2 tablespoons unsalted butter
- 2 teaspoons flour
- 1 10-ounce package frozen okra, cut into $1/2$-inch slices
- 1 large onion, chopped
- 1 32-ounce can tomatoes
- 1 bay leaf, crushed
- 2 tablespoons chopped parsley
- $1/4$ teaspoon dried thyme
- 1 tablespoon red pepper sauce
- 1 pound lump crab meat
- 4 king crab legs, cut into 2-inch pieces
- 1 quart boiling water
- 1 teaspoon gumbo filé

For the rice

- 2 cups hot cooked white rice
- 2 tablespoons unsalted butter
- $1/4$ cup (or less) chopped fresh parsley

TO MAKE THE GUMBO:

Melt the butter in a heavy stockpot. Stir in the flour. Add the okra and onion; cook until the flour is brown, stirring constantly. Add the tomatoes, bay leaf, parsley, thyme, and red pepper sauce; mix well. Simmer for 15 minutes, stirring occasionally.

Add the crab meat, crab legs, and water. Simmer, covered, for 30 minutes. Stir in the gumbo filé. Simmer until thickened, stirring frequently. Discard the bay leaf. Ladle into soup bowls.

TO MAKE THE RICE:

Combine the hot rice, butter, and parsley in a serving dish; mix lightly.

Note May prepare the gumbo ahead and freeze if desired.

Variation May substitute four cleaned and halved hard-shell crabs for the crab meat and crab legs.

SUNDRIED TOMATO LENTIL SOUP

Serves Eight

The sundried tomatoes lend a new twist to this old favorite.

Sauté the onion, celery, carrot, and garlic in the olive oil in a sauté pan until tender, stirring constantly. Add the tomato, jalapeño pepper, red pepper, and oregano; mix well. Sauté for 15 to 20 minutes or until the vegetables are tender, stirring constantly.

Add the water, bouillon cubes, and lentils; mix well. Simmer, covered, for 45 minutes or until the lentils are tender, but not mushy.

Stir in the sundried tomatoes, red pepper sauce, salt, and pepper. Ladle into soup bowls; sprinkle with the Parmesan cheese.

1 large onion, chopped

1 stalk celery, chopped

1 carrot, peeled, chopped

2–3 cloves of garlic, minced

2–4 tablespoons extra-virgin olive oil

1 tomato, seeded, chopped

1 jalapeño pepper, seeded, chopped

1/4 teaspoon crushed red pepper

1 1/2 teaspoons oregano

6–8 cups water

4 chicken bouillon cubes

1 16-ounce package lentils, sorted, rinsed

3 ounces sundried tomatoes, softened, chopped

dash of red pepper sauce

salt and freshly ground pepper to taste

grated Parmesan cheese

The multiple virtues of cast iron were discovered in the 19th century. It was cheaper than stone or brick, and it could be cast in molds into ornate shapes. Some of the finest examples of cast-iron facades, built in the 1870's, can be found on the streets of SoHo.

LEEK AND POTATO POTAGE

Serves Six

Great for a cozy afternoon by the fire or on a cold winter night.

1¹/₂ cups thinly sliced leek bulbs

2 tablespoons unsalted butter

3–4 cups chicken stock

3–4 baking potatoes, peeled, chopped

salt and freshly ground pepper to taste

¹/₄ cup milk

6 tablespoons sour cream

¹/₂ cup shredded cheddar cheese

3–4 slices cooked bacon

2–3 scallions, minced

Combine the leeks and butter in a stockpot. Cover with buttered waxed paper and "sweat" the leeks, cooking over medium heat until tender; discard the waxed paper.

Whisk in the chicken stock. Add the chopped potatoes, salt, and pepper; mix well. Bring the mixture to a boil; reduce the heat. Simmer for 30 minutes or until the potatoes are tender. Whisk in the milk.

Ladle into soup bowls. Offer the sour cream, cheddar cheese, crumbled bacon, and chopped scallions as a choice of garnishes.

Note To sweat the leeks, sauté without liquid or with minimal liquid to extract the essence. The leeks should be soft but not brown.

PUMPKIN BISQUE

Serves Four to Six

This soup could become a new Thanksgiving favorite.

¹/₂ cup unsalted butter

¹/₂ cup unbleached white flour

3 cups evaporated milk

5 cups pumpkin purée

2 cups milk

2 cups finely chopped onions

1¹/₂ bouillon cubes

1¹/₄ teaspoons sea salt

1 teaspoon ground ginger

1¹/₄ teaspoons nutmeg

toasted pumpkin seeds

Melt the butter in a large stockpot. Add the flour, stirring until blended. Cook until light brown, stirring constantly. Add the evaporated milk; mix well. Stir in the pumpkin purée and milk.

Sauté the onions in 1 tablespoon oil in a sauté pan until tender, stirring constantly. Add the onions to the pumpkin mixture; mix well. Add the bouillon cubes, sea salt, ginger, and nutmeg; mix well.

Cook until heated through, stirring constantly. Ladle into soup bowls; sprinkle with the toasted pumpkin seeds. Serve hot or cold.

Note If using fresh pumpkin, boil peeled chunks of one large pumpkin in salted water until tender, then purée.

FRENCH ONION SOUP WITH COGNAC

Serves Six

Most people enjoy a delicious bowl of onion soup. The addition of cognac gives this recipe an added kick.

Sauté the onions in the butter in a large stockpot for 20 minutes or until the onions are tender, stirring frequently. Sprinkle with the sugar. Cook until the onions are golden brown, stirring occasionally.

Add the beef stock and white wine; mix well. Bring the mixture to a boil; reduce the heat. Simmer, covered, for 1 hour. Season with the salt and pepper. Stir in the cognac.

Toast the bread slices for 10 minutes before the soup is ready. Place 1 slice of the bread in each of 6 individual ovenproof soup bowls. Pour the soup over the bread. When the bread slices float to the top, sprinkle with shredded Gruyère.

Place the soup bowls on a baking sheet. Broil until the cheese bubbles. Serve with additional French bread.

$1^3/_4$ pounds onions, thinly sliced

5 tablespoons unsalted butter

1 teaspoon sugar

$1^1/_2$ quarts beef stock

$^2/_3$ cup white wine

salt and freshly ground pepper to taste

3 tablespoons cognac

6 $^1/_2$-inch thick slices French bread

$1^1/_3$ cups shredded Gruyère cheese

COLD CURRIED AVOCADO SOUP

Serves Six

Perfect for a summer luncheon.

Combine the curry powder and a small amount of the broth in a saucepan; mix well. Simmer for 5 minutes, stirring frequently. Stir in the remaining broth.

Combine the avocado, half and half, lime juice, and onion juice in a blender container. Process until smooth. Stir into the broth mixture; season with the salt and pepper. Add additional half and half or broth if the consistency of the soup is not like heavy cream.

Chill, covered, overnight. Serve in chilled soup bowls topped with the sour cream and avocado slices.

2 teaspoons curry powder

2 cups chicken broth

1 ripe avocado, peeled

$1^1/_2$ cups half and half

2 teaspoons fresh lime juice

$^1/_2$ teaspoon onion juice

salt and freshly ground pepper to taste

sour cream

avocado slices

SPICED BUTTERNUT SQUASH SOUP

T*he toasted and spiced flavor of this soup makes it a standout! And for a low-fat treat, simply leave off the crème fraîche.*

For the crème fraîche

1/2 cup whipping cream

1/2 cup sour cream

For the soup

2 pounds butternut squash, peeled, seeded, cut into 1-inch pieces

2 carrots, peeled, cut into 1-inch slices

1 large onion, chopped

1 quart chicken broth

1/2 teaspoon nutmeg

1/2 teaspoon cinnamon

1/4 teaspoon ground ginger

1/4 teaspoon ground mace

1/4 teaspoon salt

1/4 teaspoon white pepper

toasted pumpkin seeds

TO MAKE THE CREME FRAICHE:

Combine the whipping cream and sour cream in a bowl; cover. Let stand at room temperature for 12 hours. Stir well and refrigerate for an additional 36 hours.

TO MAKE THE SOUP:

Preheat the oven to 400° F.

Combine the squash, carrots, onion, and chicken broth in a large roasting pan. Stir in the nutmeg, cinnamon, ginger, mace, salt, and white pepper. Bake, covered, for 45 to 60 minutes or until the vegetables are very tender. Cool the vegetable mixture.

Purée the mixture in a food processor. Return the purée to the roasting pan. Bring to a boil over low heat, stirring constantly.

Ladle the soup into bowls; top each serving with a dollop of the crème fraîche sprinkled with the toasted pumpkin seeds.

Note Great to prepare during busy times, since there is little stirring time...most of the cooking takes place in the oven. Freezes well, too.

BLOODY MARY GAZPACHO

Serves Twelve

This also may be served as an appetizer soup, with or without the addition of pepper vodka.

Combine the olive oil, vinegar, and tomato juice in a bowl; mix well. Seed and chop the tomatoes, bell peppers, jalapeño pepper, and cucumbers. Chop the onion, garlic, and shallots.

Process the vegetables in small batches in a food processor or blender until coarsely chopped, adding the olive oil mixture gradually.

Combine the mixture with the salt, black pepper, cayenne pepper, dill, and cilantro in a bowl; mix well. Chill for 3 hours or longer. Adjust the seasonings. Serve as the mix for Bloody Marys.

Variation Rim the glasses or bowls with jumbo shrimp for a fun first course.

1/2 cup extra-virgin olive oil
1/4 cup balsamic vinegar
1 cup vegetable or tomato juice
6–8 large ripe tomatoes
1 large red bell pepper
1 large yellow bell pepper
1 medium jalapeño pepper
2 large cucumbers
1 large purple onion
4 cloves of garlic
2–3 shallots
salt, freshly ground black pepper, and cayenne pepper to taste
1/4–1/2 cup chopped dill
1/4–1/2 cup chopped cilantro

MARTHA WASHINGTON'S PUNCH

Serves Sixteen

A great punch to add spirit to the holidays.

Combine the lemonade mix, water, brandy, Triple Sec, and cognac in a pitcher; mix well.

Combine with the champagne in a punch bowl at serving time; mix gently. Add ice.

1 6-ounce can frozen lemonade
1 6-ounce can water
1 cup apricot brandy
1 cup Triple Sec or Curaçao
2 cups cognac
2 bottles of champagne, chilled

ENTREES

MEATS
POULTRY
SEAFOOD

s the showpiece of the meal, the entrée provides the opportunity to demonstrate skill, flair and style—the hallmarks of a talented chef. The entrée is the meal's focal point. The dishes included in this chapter—meats, poultry, and seafood—constitute the full range of culinary choice.

Choose from Lincoln Center Lamb Chops or Park Avenue Pork Tenderloin, both of which take their names and tastes from neighborhoods recognized the world over for their sophistication and elegance. Try the packed-to-go selections on the *Lunch Under Sail* menu on this page for lighter fare. Sample Szechuan Spiced Shrimp or Salmon with Woven Pastry Crust, both exciting seafood entrées that are as rich and varied as the history of this great city which over 8 million people call home.

On this island that encompasses just 22 square miles, there are literally thousands of eating establishments. *A Restaurant Sampler* on page 73 offers a selection of the city's most famous kitchens. Share the secrets of some of New York's most famous chefs—let their success be yours!

During the winter holidays, there is no place on earth quite like New York. Capture the enticing blend of flavors offered on *A Holiday Celebration* menu presented on page 94.

Uptown, downtown, in a restaurant in the park, or on a sailboat on the river, New York's diversity is a joy to experience. We are sure that you will relish the diverse culinary delights that follow.

MENU

Lunch Under Sail

CRUDITES WITH TRICOLORED DIPPING SAUCES

CHICKEN WITH ORANGE AND SAGE

HARICOTS VERTS

NUTTED WILD RICE SALAD

TOMATO AND MANGO SALAD

CHOCOLATE SOUFFLE CAKE

FRUITED ICED TEA

Left overleaf, *packed to go on board, fresh flowers, crudités, Nutted Wild Rice Salad, Tomato and Mango Salad.*

Above left, *Chicken with Orange and Sage with haricots verts.*

Below left, *Nutted Wild Rice Salad with Mandarin oranges.*

Above, *a crystal ice bucket does double duty for crudités with Tricolored Dipping Sauces.*

Below, *a simple luncheon feast for the body, while the soul feasts on the views of Manhattan's downtown skyline.*

Right overleaf, *Chocolate Soufflé Cake, with its casually crumbly crust, is the ending of choice to an afternoon sail.*

PLATANOS RELLENOS

Serves Six

Rosa Mexicano, one of Manhattan's finest Mexican restaurants, provided us with this tasty entrée.

TO PREPARE THE PLANTAINS:

Dip the tomatoes briefly into boiling water or roast the tomatoes until the skin can be easily removed; remove the skin. Seed and chop the tomatoes coarsely. Set aside.

Sauté the onion and garlic in the oil in a sauté pan until tender but not brown. Increase the heat and add the tomatoes, oregano, thyme, bay leaf, salt, and pepper; mix well. Cook for 10 minutes.

Add the ground sirloin. Cook for 10 minutes, stirring until the sirloin is brown and crumbly. Remove the pan from the heat; stir in the raisins and olives; let stand until cool. Discard the bay leaf.

Cut each plantain into two 3- or 4-inch pieces. Scoop out the centers to form tubes, leaving 1/4- to 3/8-inch walls. Slice the skins carefully and remove. Spoon the sirloin mixture carefully into the plantain tubes.

Beat the egg whites in a bowl until stiff peaks form. Fold in the egg yolks. Dip each filled plantain into the mixture.

Deep-fry the plantains in hot oil, turning to brown evenly. Drain on paper towels. Serve with the tomato broth.

TO MAKE THE TOMATO BROTH:

Process the tomatoes, onion, garlic, salt, and pepper in a food processor until the mixture is coarsely ground.

Cook the mixture in the oil in a skillet over medium heat for 10 minutes. Stir in the chicken broth. Simmer for 10 minutes longer.

For the plantains

2 1/2 pounds ripe tomatoes
1 medium onion, chopped
1 clove of garlic, minced
1/4 cup vegetable oil
 pinch each of oregano and thyme
1 bay leaf
 salt and freshly ground pepper to taste
8 ounces coarsely ground sirloin
2 teaspoons (heaping) raisins, plumped
10 pitted olives, cut into quarters
6 very ripe (black) plantains, unpeeled
6 egg whites
5 egg yolks
 oil for deep frying

For the tomato broth

2 tomatoes, peeled
1 small onion
1 clove of garlic, sliced
 salt and freshly ground pepper to taste
3 tablespoons vegetable oil
1–1 1/2 cups chicken broth

MEATS **57**

STUFFED BEEF TOURNEDOS

Serves Four

A *hearty main course.*

2 ounces mixed dried shiitake and porcini mushrooms

1 shallot, chopped

1 tablespoon chopped fresh oregano or 1 teaspoon dried oregano

3 tablespoons unsalted butter

4 6-ounce beef tenderloin steaks, 1 inch thick

salt and freshly ground pepper to taste

1/2 cup cabernet sauvignon

Combine the mushrooms with water to cover in a bowl; weight to hold the mushrooms under the water. Microwave on high for 4 minutes or let stand at room temperature for 30 minutes. Strain, reserving 1/2 cup of the liquid. Slice the mushrooms, discarding the tough stems.

Sauté the mushrooms, shallot, and oregano in 1 tablespoon butter in a sauté pan for 2 minutes or until the vegetables are tender, stirring occasionally.

Cut a horizontal pocket in one side of each steak. Spoon the mushroom mixture into the steaks.

Cook the steaks in a heated sauté pan over medium heat for 3 minutes on each side or until medium-rare. Remove to a warm platter; season with salt and pepper.

Increase the heat to high. Add the wine to the sauté pan, stirring to deglaze. Cook for 1 minute, stirring constantly. Stir in the reserved mushroom liquid.

Cook until the liquid is reduced to 1/4 cup. Whisk in the remaining 2 tablespoons butter. Serve over steaks.

Note Six ounces of fresh wild mushrooms may be substituted for dried mushrooms; use beef stock for the mushroom liquid.

STEAK WITH GARLIC CREAM SAUCE

Serves Six

This sauce is superb with either steak or broiled lamb chops. Its flavors from wine and cognac are smoothed out by the garlic-flavored cream, more sweet than sharp since the garlic is roasted.

Preheat the oven to 350° F.

Sprinkle the steaks with salt and pepper. Let stand at room temperature while making the garlic cream.

Place the unpeeled cloves of garlic on a baking sheet. Roast for 10 minutes or until very soft. Let stand until cool enough to handle.

Squeeze the cloves of garlic out of their skins. Purée with the cream in the food processor; set aside.

Heat the butter in a sauté pan over high heat. Add the steaks. Sear on both sides. Cook until the steaks are medium-rare or until done to taste. Remove to a warm plate.

Flambé the pan with the cognac. Add the wine, stirring to deglaze the pan. Stir in the veal stock. Cook until reduced by half.

Stir in the garlic cream. Simmer for 5 minutes. Adjust the seasonings. Spoon the garlic cream sauce over the steaks to serve.

6 10-ounce New York strip steaks

salt and freshly ground pepper to taste

8 cloves of garlic, unpeeled

1/2 cup heavy cream

1/4 cup unsalted butter

2 tablespoons cognac

1/4 cup dry white wine

1 1/2 cups veal or beef stock

ROULADE OF BEEF

Serves Four

From *Café des Artistes, the full name of this recipe is Roulade of Beef, Austrian Housewife Style. Executive Chef Thomas Ferlesch, who was born in Vienna, remembers this typical Austrian and German dish from his childhood. It has since migrated from home kitchens to well-known European restaurants, where it is called Rindsroulade Nach Hausfrauen Art. It fits comfortably on the Café's bourgeois menu, where it is served with kohlrabi, carrots, new potatoes, or, in the winter, spatzle.*

Preheat the oven to 375° F.

Sauté the onions in 1 tablespoon of the oil in a sauté pan for 5 minutes or just until translucent. Remove the sautéed onions with a slotted spoon.

Place the beef on a large work surface. Spread each paillard with mustard; sprinkle with the 1 teaspoon salt and ¾ teaspoon pepper. Sprinkle the onions evenly over each paillard; arrange the pickle slices lengthwise over the beef. Place 1 slice of the bacon on each paillard. Roll the beef tightly to enclose the filling and tie securely in 3 places.

Coat the rolls well with the flour, shaking off the excess. Sear the rolls in the remaining 2 tablespoons oil in a heated medium heavy ovenproof sauté pan until they are brown on all sides; drain. Add the water to the sauté pan and reduce the heat to medium-high. Cook for 5 minutes, stirring to deglaze the pan. Add the stock, sour cream, red wine, tomato paste, and paprika.

Bake, uncovered, for 45 minutes. Remove the beef roulades to a serving plate; remove the string.

Strain the cooking liquid into a saucepan. Simmer the liquid until it is reduced to a consistency which will coat the back of a spoon. Season to taste with the sugar, salt, and pepper. Serve with the beef roulades.

Note The beef roulades may be chilled in the sauce and reheated on top of the stove or in a 300-degree oven.

2 medium onions, cut into quarters

3 tablespoons vegetable oil

4 11-ounce paillards of top or bottom beef round, pounded thin

2 tablespoons Dijon mustard

1 teaspoon salt

¾ teaspoon freshly ground pepper

1 large kosher dill pickle, thinly sliced lengthwise

4 slices bacon

¼ cup flour

2 cups water

2 cups chicken or beef stock

1 cup sour cream

1 cup dry red wine

1½ tablespoons tomato paste

2 tablespoons Hungarian paprika

sugar, salt, and freshly ground pepper to taste

"Give me your tired, your poor,

Your huddled masses yearning to breathe free."

from **The New Colossus** *by Emma Lazarus, engraved on the base of the Statue of Liberty.*

STEAK SHERROD

A *very quick and easy choice for a delectable meal.*

6 scallions with tops, chopped

3 tablespoons unsalted butter

2 tablespoons worcestershire sauce

freshly ground pepper to taste

1 3-pound London broil

Melba toast rounds

As the jib is lowered on the East River, the lower Manhattan skyline comes into view. Shown here are One New York Plaza and 55 Water Street.

Sauté the scallions in the butter in a sauté pan until golden brown. Add the worcestershire sauce and pepper. Keep warm over low heat.

Grill the beef until done to taste. Cut into thin slices.

Place the beef slices on Melba toast rounds. Top with the sauce.

Variation Use sirloin steak as a substitute for London broil.

WARM PEPPERED FILLET OF BEEF

Serves Six to Eight

This dish can be served hot, warm, or cold. Carve it into thin slices and serve it with the horseradish cream.

TO PREPARE THE BEEF:

Preheat the oven and broiler pan to 425° F.

Rub the beef with the olive oil. Crush the pink peppercorns. Mix the crushed peppercorns with the black pepper and tarragon in a small bowl. Press the mixture over the surface of the beef. Sprinkle generously with the salt.

Place the beef on the heated broiler pan, turning to sear on all sides. Roast to 125° F. on the meat thermometer for medium-rare. Let stand for several minutes before slicing.

TO MAKE THE HORSERADISH CREAM:

Combine the garlic and horseradish in a food processor container; process until minced. Add the cream gradually, processing constantly until the mixture is thick and smooth, scraping the bowl.

Add the vinegar, worcestershire sauce, and red pepper sauce; process for 5 seconds. Season to taste with salt. Serve with the beef.

Variation Serve on French bread for an hors d'oeuvre as seen on page 20. Or, use leftovers in a marinated steak salad.

For the beef

- 1 3- to 4-pound fillet of beef, trimmed, tied
- 1/4 cup olive oil
- 1/4 cup pink peppercorns
- 1/4 cup coarsely cracked black pepper
- 1/4 cup tarragon leaves
  kosher salt

For the horseradish cream

- 1 medium clove of garlic
- 1 1½-by-1½-inch piece of fresh horseradish
- 1 cup heavy cream, chilled
- 2 teaspoons red wine vinegar
- 1 teaspoon worcestershire sauce
- 3 drops of red pepper sauce
  salt to taste

CURRIED MEAT LOAF WITH GINGER

Serves Four to Six

Deviating from the norm, curry, ginger, and carrot add a spicy flair to this classic favorite.

½ cup bread crumbs

1 large egg

1 tablespoon olive oil

2 small chopped onions

1 clove of garlic, minced

1 tablespoon curry powder

1 tablespoon ground cumin

1 tablespoon ginger

1 cup shredded carrots

½ pound lean ground beef

1 pound lean ground lamb

½ pound lean ground pork

The skyline of Manhattan from Brooklyn Heights includes One Financial Square and 120 Wall Street on either side of the Citibank building, all towering over the South Street Seaport to the north, on the right in this picture.

Preheat the oven to 350° F.

Combine the bread crumbs, egg, and olive oil in a bowl; mix well. Add the onions and garlic; mix well. Sprinkle the curry powder, cumin, and ginger over the bread crumb mixture; mix lightly.

Add the carrots and the ground beef, ground lamb, and ground pork. Mix lightly until the mixture is well combined.

Pat into a 5-by-9-inch loaf pan or shape into a loaf in a baking pan. Bake the meat loaf for 1 hour.

Note Serve with basmati rice.

LINCOLN CENTER LAMB CHOPS

Serves Four

Mint butter makes these lamb chops special, and they are great to serve when time is of the essence.

Combine the mint, butter, lemon juice, salt, and pepper in a bowl; mix until smooth. Chill for 10 minutes.

Preheat the broiler.

Score the lamb chops on each side with a sharp knife. Reserve 4 teaspoons of the mint butter. Spread the remaining mint butter on the lamb chops.

Place the lamb chops on the rack in a broiler pan. Broil for 4 to 5 minutes on each side or until done to taste. Serve with the reserved mint butter.

2 tablespoons chopped fresh mint

1/2 cup unsalted butter, softened

1 teaspoon fresh lemon juice

1/4 teaspoon salt

freshly ground pepper to taste

4 1 1/2-inch thick loin lamb chops

MARINATED ROLLED LAMB

E*legant and particularly good for beginner cooks or those in a rush.*

1 cup Dijon mustard

2 tablespoons soy sauce

2 tablespoons vegetable oil

1 tablespoon rosemary

¼ teaspoon ginger

1 6-pound leg of lamb, boned, rolled

Combine the mustard, soy sauce, oil, rosemary, and ginger in a bowl; mix well. Brush on the lamb.

Place in a roasting pan. Marinate in the refrigerator for 8 hours. Preheat the oven to 350° F.

Roast the lamb for 1¼ hours or until done to taste, basting with the marinade.

Note Ask your butcher to bone and roll the leg of lamb.

ORANGE ROSEMARY LAMB STEW

Serves Six to Eight

This hearty stew recipe is a favorite from Tavern on the Green. Great for those cold wintery nights.

Cut the lamb into 1½-inch cubes. Brown the cubes in the peanut oil in a heavy saucepan; drain. Add the carrots, onion, garlic, celery, thyme, and rosemary to the lamb. Sauté for 10 minutes, stirring frequently.

Sprinkle with the flour. Cook for 10 minutes, but do not brown. Add the wine, liqueur, orange juice, and orange peel; mix gently. Season with the salt and pepper.

Cook for 30 minutes or until the mixture is reduced by half. Stir in the chicken stock. Cook over medium heat for 1½ hours or until the lamb is tender.

Remove the pith from the orange sections. Cut into small segments. Sprinkle the orange segments over the lamb just before serving the stew.

*At left, a wide variety of historic ships is berthed in the slips at the South Street Seaport. This ship, the **Peking**, was built in 1911. It is the second largest sailing ship and one of the last sailing vessels used for cargo shipment.*

2½ pounds boneless lamb shoulder, trimmed

¼ cup peanut oil

3 carrots, chopped

1 large onion, chopped

1 clove of garlic, minced

3 stalks celery, chopped

1 tablespoon fresh thyme

1 tablespoon fresh rosemary

1 tablespoon flour

2 cups dry white wine

¼ cup Grand Marnier

1 cup fresh orange juice

3 tablespoons julienned orange peel, blanched

coarse salt and freshly ground pepper to taste

2 cups chicken stock

1 small orange, peeled, sectioned

GRILLED BUTTERFLIED LEG OF LAMB

Butterflied leg of lamb is always a favorite and easy to cook on an outdoor barbecue.

For the marinade

2 cups peanut oil

1/2 cup fresh lemon juice

4 cloves of garlic, pressed

8 dashes (or more) of worcestershire sauce

4 sprigs of fresh rosemary

2 teaspoons fresh oregano

6 dashes of red pepper sauce

1/2 cup soy sauce

For the lamb

6 large onions, sliced

1 6- to 7-pound leg of lamb, boned, butterflied, trimmed

1/2 bunch fresh parsley

TO MAKE THE MARINADE:

Combine the peanut oil, lemon juice, garlic, worcestershire sauce, rosemary, oregano, red pepper sauce, and soy sauce in a bowl; mix well.

TO PREPARE THE LAMB:

Spread the onions in a shallow dish; place the lamb over the onions. Pour the marinade over the lamb. Marinate in the refrigerator for 2 to 8 hours. Drain, reserving the marinade.

Preheat the grill.

Grill the lamb for about 20 minutes for medium-rare or until done to taste, checking thinner sections first to judge degree of doneness, basting with the reserved marinade. Heat the remaining reserved marinade in a saucepan. Serve with the lamb. Garnish with the fresh parsley.

Note Make sure that all of the fat is trimmed from the lamb and have water ready to douse the flames on the grill, because the fat and the oil in the marinade can cause the coals to flare up. Lamb may need to be cut into sections for even cooking.

LAMB WITH HERB-HAZELNUT CRUST

Serves Ten

A *showstopper that gets more raves than Broadway.*

Preheat the oven to 350° F. Process the hazelnuts in a food processor until coarsely chopped. Cream the butter in a bowl. Add the hazelnuts, bread crumbs, garlic, and rosemary; mix well.

Season the lamb with salt and pepper; place it in a roasting pan. Pack the hazelnut mixture evenly over the lamb, allowing some to drop into the pan. Roast for 1¼ to 1½ hours or until meat thermometer registers 130° for medium-rare.

Note Use the pan juices to make a flavorful gravy.

1 cup hazelnuts, roasted, skinned

½ cup unsalted butter, softened

1 cup fine dry bread crumbs

3 cloves of garlic, finely chopped

3 tablespoons chopped fresh rosemary

1 6- to 7-pound leg of lamb
salt and freshly ground pepper to taste

KARSKY SHASHLIK SUPREME

Serves Four

T *his lamb recipe is from the Russian Tea Room. Shashlik originated with the Mongols, who skewered their meat on swords and roasted succulent lamb over open flames. Before Ivan the Terrible drove them out of Russia during the sixteenth century, he preempted their Shashlik. The dish eventually found its way to Moscow restaurants, where the meat was marinated overnight, then cooked in its own juices.*

Combine the peanut oil, onion, lemon juice, brandy, garlic, parsley, salt, and pepper in a stainless steel bowl; mix well.

Add the lamb or other meat to the marinade. Marinate, covered, in the refrigerator for 8 hours to overnight, turning occasionally. Drain, reserving the marinade.

Roast or grill the meat until done to taste, basting with the reserved marinade.

1 cup peanut oil

6 ounces finely chopped onion

2 tablespoons fresh lemon juice

1 tablespoon brandy

1 tablespoon minced garlic

2 tablespoons chopped fresh parsley

1 teaspoon salt

1 teaspoon freshly ground pepper

1 whole loin of lamb, fully trimmed

PORK CHOPS KORMA

Serve this with homemade pappadums, which are easy to make with a mix available at specialty food stores. The menu might also include cucumber raita, which is a mixture of yogurt and chopped cucumbers, basmati or saffron rice, and an Indian bread such as naan.

6 1-inch thick pork loin or center-cut chops

1/2 teaspoon each salt and freshly ground pepper

1 tablespoon olive oil

1 8-ounce can tomato sauce

1/2 cup catsup or chili sauce

1/2 teaspoon onion salt

1 bay leaf

1/4 teaspoon curry powder

fresh parsley

Season the pork chops with the salt and pepper. Brown the chops in the olive oil in a sauté pan for about 5 minutes on each side.

Combine the tomato sauce, catsup, onion salt, bay leaf, and curry powder in a bowl; mix well. Pour over the pork chops. Simmer, covered, for 45 minutes or until tender; discard the bay leaf.

Garnish with the fresh parsley.

Note Pappadums are tortilla-like breads made with lentil flour. They are an East Indian specialty.

PARK AVENUE PORK TENDERLOIN

Pork tenderloin is a healthy alternative to chicken breasts and is very quick and easy to prepare.

1 cup soy sauce

2 tablespoons honey

1/2 cup vodka

1/2 cup bourbon

1 1- to 1 1/2-pound pork tenderloin

pepper jelly or chutney

1 baguette, sliced

Preheat the oven to 325° F.

Combine the soy sauce, honey, vodka, and bourbon in a shallow dish; mix well. Add the pork. Marinate in the refrigerator for 4 hours or overnight.

Remove the pork to a baking pan. Bake, covered, for 30 minutes or grill. Serve with pepper jelly or chutney.

Variation Cut pork into 1/4-inch slices and serve with the suggested condiments on baguette rounds.

PEANUT MARINATED PORK SKEWERS
Serves Four to Six

Peanuts add an innovative twist to a traditional shish kabob.

TO MAKE THE MARINADE:

Combine the oil, soy sauce, peanuts, worcestershire sauce, onion, garlic, brown sugar, and curry powder in a bowl; mix well.

TO MAKE THE PORK SKEWERS:

Cut the pork into ½-inch slices. Combine it with the marinade in a shallow dish. Marinate, covered, in the refrigerator for 1 hour.

Preheat the oven to 450° F.

Drain the pork, reserving the marinade. Alternate the pork, mushrooms, peppers, and zucchini on skewers; place in a roasting pan. Broil or grill for 10 to 15 minutes or until the pork is cooked through, turning occasionally and basting with the reserved marinade.

Variation Substitute chicken or beef for the pork if preferred.

For the marinade

½ cup vegetable oil

¼ cup soy sauce

3 tablespoons chopped peanuts

2 tablespoons worcestershire sauce

2 tablespoons chopped onion

3 cloves of garlic, crushed

1 tablespoon brown sugar

½ teaspoon curry powder

For the pork skewers

3 pounds boneless pork

8 medium mushrooms

1 green bell pepper, cut into 1-inch pieces

1 red bell pepper, cut into 1-inch pieces

1 medium zucchini, peeled, cut into ½-inch pieces

DILLED VEAL WITH CREME FRAICHE

An elegantly rich entrée for your next dinner party.

For the crème fraîche

½ cup whipping cream

½ cup sour cream

For the dilled veal

1½ pounds veal scallops, cut into 1-inch pieces

4 tablespoons unsalted butter

1 large onion, chopped

2 cloves of garlic, minced

8 ounces mushrooms, sliced

3 medium carrots, grated

2 shallots, finely chopped

¼ cup dry white wine

3 tablespoons flour

½ teaspoon dill

10 ounces chicken broth

TO MAKE THE CREME FRAICHE:

Combine the whipping cream and sour cream in a bowl; cover. Let stand at room temperature for 12 hours. Stir well and refrigerate for an additional 36 hours.

TO PREPARE THE DILLED VEAL:

Sauté the veal in 2 tablespoons of the butter in a sauté pan until veal loses its pink color; do not overcook. Remove the veal to a bowl.

Add the onion, garlic, mushrooms, carrots, shallots, and remaining 2 tablespoons butter to the sauté pan. Cook until the vegetables are tender, stirring frequently. Stir in the wine.

Cook until the wine evaporates. Stir in the flour. Cook for 2 minutes, stirring constantly. Add the dill and chicken broth. Cook for 2 minutes. Add the crème fraîche and veal. Cook just until heated through; do not boil. Serve over rice or noodles.

Left overleaf, *a sybarite's delight ...*
breakfast in the Museum Suite at Manhattan's
Stanhope Hotel features
Banana Macadamia Waffles, fresh fruit,
and chilled champagne.

Left above, *Central Park sparkles with*
thousands of twinkling lights that wrap the
trees surrounding Tavern on the Green.

Far left below, *Orange Rosemary Lamb Stew*
is the perfect version of an old classic.

Near left below, *the table is set with the first*
course and awaiting the guests ...
Sautéed Foie Gras with polenta crescents
and lady apples.

Right above, *a romantic dinner at*
Café des Artistes ...leaded windows, painted
murals, subdued colors make this
one of Manhattan's most intimate venues.

Right below, *Crisp Scallop and*
Salmon Cakes served with farmhouse potatoes.

Below, *the contemporary cuisine of Bouley brings us
Maine Day-Boat Lobster with a trio of colorful sauces.*

VEAL CHOPS WITH PORT SAUCE

T*he port and mushrooms make this a sophisticated choice for last-minute guests.*

Sauté the veal chops in the butter in a large sauté pan for 10 minutes on each side. Place the chops on an ovenproof platter; keep warm in a warm oven.

Add the mushrooms to the drippings in the sauté pan. Sauté for 3 minutes. Stir in the wine, chicken stock, and cream. Bring to a boil. Cook until thickened, stirring constantly.

Spoon the sauce over the veal chops. Sprinkle with the pepper and chopped parsley.

4 veal shoulder chops

4 tablespoons unsalted butter

1½ cups sliced mushrooms

2 tablespoons port

½ cup chicken stock

½ cup heavy cream

freshly ground pepper to taste

1 tablespoon chopped parsley

VEAL FONTAL

Here is a dish that can be prepared quickly, looks elegant and is full of flavor.

4 1½-inch thick veal chops

1 tablespoon unsalted butter

1 tablespoon olive oil

¼ cup white wine

¼ teaspoon sage

salt and freshly ground pepper to taste

8 ounces fontina cheese, cut into 4 equal slices

Remove the long chop bone from the veal chops. Brown the chops on both sides in a mixture of the butter and olive oil in a sauté pan over medium heat.

Add the wine to the sauté pan, stirring to deglaze. Add the sage, salt, and pepper to taste. Simmer, covered, for 10 to 15 minutes for medium-rare or until done to taste.

Remove the chops from the sauté pan. Cut a lengthwise pocket in each chop with a sharp knife. Insert a cheese slice into each chop. Return to sauté pan and simmer for 2 to 3 minutes. Place the chops on a serving plate; spoon the remaining sauce from the sauté pan over the top.

Variation Goat cheese may be substituted for fontina. However, be sure to add more seasonings. Try adding thyme, rosemary, basil or sundried tomatoes, and garlic.

Serves Eight

W*hen sliced, this veal looks delightful.*

TO MAKE THE STUFFING:

Rinse the spinach; drain. Remove the stems and tough center veins in the larger leaves. Cook the spinach in a small amount of water in a saucepan until tender; drain and cool, squeezing to remove excess moisture. Chop the spinach fine.

Combine the spinach with the ground beef, ground pork, and parsley in a bowl; mix well. Add the eggs, cheese, salt, pepper, and nutmeg; mix well.

TO COOK THE VEAL ROAST:

Preheat the oven to 400° F.

Open out the veal roast on a work surface; sprinkle with the salt. Spread the spinach mixture to within 1/2 inch of the edges. Roll the veal roast to enclose the filling. Secure with string.

Brush the roll with olive oil; place the veal roast in a baking pan just large enough to hold the veal roast. Sprinkle the celery, carrot, onion, garlic, rosemary, and sage around the veal roast. Dot with the butter.

Roast for 1 1/2 hours, turning the veal roast 4 or 5 times and basting with the wine. Remove the veal roast to a serving plate, discarding the string.

Skim the pan juices into a saucepan. Stir in a mixture of the chicken broth and cornstarch. Simmer until thickened, stirring constantly. Serve with the veal roast.

For the stuffing

12 ounces fresh spinach

4 ounces lean ground beef

4 ounces ground pork

chopped flat parsley to taste

2 eggs

3/4 cup grated Parmesan cheese

salt, freshly ground pepper, and nutmeg to taste

For the veal roast

1 3-pound breast of veal roast, boned

salt to taste

1 tablespoon olive oil

2 stalks celery, chopped

1 medium carrot, chopped

1 small onion, chopped

3 cloves of garlic, crushed

rosemary and sage to taste

2 tablespoons unsalted butter

1/2 cup dry white wine

6 tablespoons chicken broth

1/2 teaspoon cornstarch

VENISON MEDALLIONS

Serves Four

Venison is a red meat that is low in fat and cholesterol. The gamey flavor of the venison is complemented by a mushroom sauce. Serve with Nutted Wild Rice for a colorful presentation.

TO MAKE THE MUSHROOM SAUCE:

Melt the butter with the olive oil and wine in a sauté pan. Add the shallots and mushrooms. Cook just until the shallots are tender. Add the broth. Simmer until the sauce is reduced to ⅔ cup; keep warm.

TO PREPARE THE VENISON MEDALLIONS:

Coat the medallions with the flour, shaking off the excess; sprinkle with the pepper.

Heat the butter and olive oil in a nonstick sauté pan over high heat. Add the medallions. Sauté quickly just until brown on the outside and still pink on the inside. Remove to a heated platter.

Add the wine to the sauté pan, stirring to deglaze the sauté pan. Add the mushroom sauce; mix well. Stir in the half and half; adjust the seasonings.

Spoon the sauce onto serving plates. Place the medallions in or beside the sauce; garnish with the rosemary. Serve immediately.

Note Venison is deer meat. Elk meat can also be used. Both are available at specialty butcher shops or by mail from South Millbrook Venison Products in Millbrook, New York.

The Sherry Netherland Hotel was built during Manhattan's gilded age in the French Beaux Arts style. Its clock is a well-known landmark on Fifth Avenue.

For the mushroom sauce

- 1 tablespoon unsalted butter or margarine
- 1 tablespoon olive oil or canola oil
- ¼ cup red wine
- 1–2 shallots, chopped
- 8 small boletes or other fresh wild mushrooms, cut into halves
- 1 cup game broth or low-salt canned beef broth

For the venison medallions

- 8–12 venison medallions
- flour
- freshly ground pepper to taste
- 2–3 tablespoons unsalted butter or margarine
- 2–3 tablespoons olive oil or canola oil
- ¼ cup wine or broth
- ½ cup half and half
- sprig of rosemary

SPA STYLE CHICKEN ENCHILADAS

Serve these with pico de gallo or black bean and corn salsa for a southwestern dinner.

3 onions, finely chopped

2 cloves of garlic, finely chopped

2 tablespoons chili powder

1 teaspoon ground cumin

1 teaspoon salt

1 28-ounce can tomatoes

2 cups chopped cooked chicken

1 cup shredded low-fat sharp cheddar cheese

8 corn tortillas

Preheat the oven to 350° F.

Cook the onions and garlic in a nonstick saucepan over very low heat until tender, stirring frequently.

Add the chili powder, cumin, and salt. Drain the juice from the tomatoes into the saucepan. Chop the tomatoes and add to the saucepan; mix well. Simmer, covered, for 10 minutes.

Pour half of the sauce into a bowl and reserve.

Add the chicken and half the cheese to the remaining sauce in the saucepan; mix well.

Spoon the chicken mixture onto the center of each tortilla; roll the tortilla to enclose the filling. Place the enchiladas seam side down in a baking dish.

Spoon the reserved sauce over the enchiladas; sprinkle with the remaining cheese. Bake, covered, for 30 minutes.

Note The tortillas for this recipe need to be soaked in water or chicken broth before they are filled to prevent cracking. The amount of chili powder can be adjusted to achieve the desired level of spiciness; add one more tablespoon of chili powder for moderate spiciness.

BALSAMIC CHICKEN BREASTS

Serves Four

Balsamic vinegar and porcini mushrooms combine to make this chicken an elegant meal which is simple to prepare.

Rinse the chicken and pat dry. Sprinkle with the salt and pepper.

Dredge the chicken in a mixture of the flour, salt, and pepper; shake off the excess flour.

Cook the fillets in the olive oil in a sauté pan over medium-high heat for 3 minutes on one side or until brown. Add the garlic.

Turn the chicken over; sprinkle with the mushrooms. Cook for 3 minutes, shaking the sauté pan to redistribute the mushrooms so they will cook evenly.

Stir in the balsamic vinegar, chicken stock, and wine. Cook, covered, over medium-low heat for 10 minutes, turning the chicken occasionally.

4 boneless chicken breasts, split

salt and freshly ground pepper to taste

2 tablespoons flour

2 tablespoons olive oil or 1 tablespoon olive oil and 1 tablespoon unsalted butter

3 cloves of garlic, minced

8 ounces porcini mushrooms

1/4 cup balsamic vinegar

3/4 cup chicken stock

3 tablespoons white wine

CHICKEN WITH ORANGE AND SAGE

Serves Four to Six

A light and easy luncheon or dinner entrée that can be served hot or cold.

Preheat the oven to 375° F.

Split the chicken breasts into halves. Trim off the excess fat, rinse, and pat dry. Sprinkle with the salt and pepper. Place on a lightly oiled baking pan.

Place a sage leaf under and on top of each piece of chicken. Drizzle with the orange juice.

Place a sheet of oiled waxed paper directly on the chicken. Bake for 10 to 12 minutes or until cooked through. Cool in the pan.

Slice the chicken and arrange alternating with orange slices on a serving plate. Reduce the pan juices in a saucepan. Stir in the marmalade. Cook until thickened. Spoon over the chicken.

4 boneless chicken breasts

salt and freshly ground pepper to taste

1 bunch fresh sage

1 cup fresh orange juice

2 navel oranges, thinly sliced

4 teaspoons orange marmalade

CRISPY CHICKEN UNDER A BRICK

Serves Four

Crispy Chicken Cooked Under a Brick with Lemon and Herbs *is the full name of this recipe. It comes to us from Chef Daniel Boulud at the restaurant Daniel, on the East Side of Manhattan. Olive oil with thyme, lemon, garlic, and chives accents this light and incredibly tasty version of the traditional chicken crisped under a brick. The mattone is the earthenware brick used in the Lucca region of Tuscany, Italy, and it is essential, as its weight is the main reason the chicken develops its tantalizingly crisp crust. Serve it with roasted seasonal vegetables or a young lettuce and herb salad tossed with a lemon dressing.*

2 2½-pound free-range
 chickens

4 cloves of garlic, cut into
 quarters lengthwise

3 sprigs of fresh rosemary

3 sprigs of fresh thyme

 salt and crushed
 peppercorns to taste

¼ cup plus 2 tablespoons olive
 oil

2 lemons, sliced ¼ inch thick

2 tablespoons fresh lemon juice

¼ cup ½-inch chive pieces

Left overleaf, the massed flags of all the member nations of the United Nations encircle the skating rink at Rockefeller Center, west of Fifth Avenue between 49th and 50th Streets.

At right, the Tavern on the Green restaurant at Central Park West and 67th Street is surrounded all year by trees festooned with tiny white lights.

Cut each chicken into halves, discarding the giblets and excess fat. Pound on the skin side with a meat mallet to flatten. Rinse the chicken halves and pat dry. Stud the chicken breasts and legs with the garlic and with 1 sprig each of the rosemary and thyme. Season it with the salt and peppercorns.

Combine the chicken halves with the ¼ cup olive oil, lemon slices, and remaining rosemary and thyme in a bowl; mix well. Marinate in the refrigerator for 5 hours to overnight.

Preheat the oven to 475° F.

Heat 1 or 2 cast-iron skillets over high heat. Add 1 tablespoon of the olive oil. Place the chicken halves skin side down in the cast-iron skillet. Add the lemon slices and marinating herbs.

Wrap 2 bricks or flat heavy stones with foil; place the bricks over the chicken halves. Cook for 8 to 10 minutes or until the chicken halves are evenly brown.

Place the cast-iron skillet in the oven. Roast the chicken halves for 20 minutes. Remove the bricks and turn the chicken halves. Roast for 10 to 15 minutes longer or until cooked through. Place the chicken on a large platter. Garnish with the roasted lemon slices and herbs. Sprinkle with the lemon juice, the remaining 1 tablespoon of olive oil, and the chives. Serve immediately, while hot and crispy.

Serves Eight to Ten

A luxurious dish full of artichoke hearts and mushrooms, with a tease of fresh tarragon.

Preheat the oven to 350° F.

Rinse the chicken and pat dry. Season with the paprika, salt, and pepper. Sauté the chicken on both sides in ½ cup of the butter in a sauté pan until brown.

Place the chicken in a baking pan; top with the artichoke hearts.

Combine the mushrooms, remaining ½ cup butter, and tarragon in a sauté pan. Sauté the mushrooms for 5 minutes, stirring occasionally. Stir in the flour. Add the sherry and the chicken stock; mix well. Simmer for 5 minutes, stirring frequently. Pour over the chicken and artichoke hearts.

Bake, covered, for 45 minutes.

Note Clarify the butter by melting the butter and skimming off the foamy milk solids. The remaining butter can be heated to very high temperatures without burning. Two cups of butter will yield a cup of clarified butter.

6 boneless chicken breasts, split

paprika to taste

salt and freshly ground pepper to taste

1 cup clarified unsalted butter

2 15-ounce cans artichoke hearts, drained

1 pound mushrooms, sliced

¼ teaspoon tarragon

6 tablespoons flour

1 cup dry sherry

3 cups chicken stock

HERB-ROASTED CHICKEN

Serves Four

F*resh herbs heighten the flavor of this traditional roasted chicken.*

Preheat the oven to 400° F.

Rinse the chicken and pat dry. Rub the chicken cavity with the salt, pepper, and lemon juice. Fill the cavity with the apple, onion, celery and 3/4 of the herbs; truss with a butcher's string.

Place the chicken breast side up in a heavy roasting pan. Roast for 15 minutes.

Arrange the shallots and garlic around the chicken. Reserve a few of the herbs for garnish. Add the remaining herbs. Pour the white wine over the chicken, shallots, and garlic. Roast for 1 to 1½ hours or until the legs move easily and the juices run clear when the chicken is pierced with a fork.

Place the chicken on a serving platter, surrounded by the shallots and garlic. Garnish with the reserved herbs.

The Plaza Hotel, an Edwardian masterpiece designed by Henry J. Harden-bergh, was completed in 1907 for the outlandish sum of $12.5 million. The cast-iron structure has classic lightposts from an earlier era that frame the doorway.

1 4- to 5-pound roasting chicken

salt and freshly ground pepper to taste

2 tablespoons fresh lemon juice

1 apple, quartered

1 onion, quartered

1 stalk celery, cut into large pieces

10 sprigs of thyme, chopped

6 sprigs of fresh rosemary, chopped

6 sage leaves, chopped

16 shallots, peeled

6 cloves of garlic, unpeeled

1/2 cup white wine

GRILLED PECHUGAS DE POLLO

C hock-full of flavor and spices, this chicken will be a favorite, year-round, on the stove or grill.

6 boneless chicken breasts, split

1 cup olive oil

1/2 cup fresh lime juice

1/2 cup honey

1/4 cup chopped cilantro

2 jalapeño peppers, seeded, chopped

4 cloves of garlic, minced

1 1/2 teaspoons ground cumin

1 tablespoon oregano

kosher salt to taste

freshly ground black pepper to taste

cayenne pepper to taste

red pepper sauce to taste

red pepper flakes to taste

2 tablespoons dark rum

mango pico de gallo
(see page 91)

tomatillo sauce
(see page 91)

Rinse the chicken and pat dry. Arrange the chicken in a shallow baking dish.

Combine the olive oil and lime juice in a bowl. Beat with a wire whisk until blended. Add the honey; mix well. Stir in the cilantro, jalapeño peppers, garlic, cumin, oregano, kosher salt, black pepper, cayenne pepper, red pepper sauce, red pepper flakes, and dark rum. Pour the mixture over the chicken, turning to coat. Marinate, covered, in the refrigerator for 1 hour to overnight.

Preheat the grill. Grill the chicken breasts over hot coals for 5 to 7 minutes on each side or until the chicken is tender. Nap the serving dish with the Mango Pico de Gallo. Arrange the chicken breasts on top. Spoon the Tomatillo Sauce over the chicken breasts. Sprinkle with red pepper flakes and rum.

Note May broil the chicken indoors in a cast-iron skillet with ridges or on a grilling pan.

MANGO PICO DE GALLO

Serves Twelve

Although this sauce was designed to accompany Grilled Pechugas de Pollo, it may be used with tortillas or to add flavor and interest to a wide variety of grilled fish.

Combine the tomatoes, mango, onion, oregano, garlic, jalapeño peppers, green chilies, and cilantro in a glass dish. Add the lime juice and vinegar; toss to mix well. Chill, covered, overnight.

Note Mango Pico de Gallo is better if made one day ahead.

2 cups chopped seeded tomatoes with liquid

1 mango, peeled, diced

1 medium onion, chopped

1 teaspoon oregano

2 cloves of garlic, minced

2 tablespoons minced jalapeño peppers

1 4-ounce can chopped green chilies or chilinis, drained

1/4 cup chopped cilantro leaves

2 tablespoons each fresh lime juice and white wine vinegar

TOMATILLO SAUCE

Serves Twelve

Tomatillos belong to the tomato family and are also related to the cape gooseberry. Their flavor has hints of lemon, apple, and herbs.

Combine the tomatillos, jalapeño peppers, green chilies, avocado, garlic, cilantro, and salt in a bowl; mix well. Serve the sauce with chicken or fish.

Note Tomatillos are the small green tomatoes that are available in specialty markets. Choose firm tomatillos, check them carefully at the store, and use them as soon as possible because they bruise and spoil easily. Remove husks before cooking. If fresh tomatillos are unavailable, use drained canned tomatillos.

12 tomatillos, chopped

1-3 jalapeño peppers, seeded, chopped

1 4-ounce can chopped green chilies, drained

1 large avocado, cubed

1 clove of garlic, minced

1/4 cup chopped cilantro

1/2 teaspoon salt

CHICKEN POTPIE

Some old favorites never go out of style. Serve this wonderful dish at a pre-matinee brunch or a post-opera supper.

1/4 cup unsalted butter

6 tablespoons flour

1 cup milk

2 cups chicken broth or 1 cup chicken broth and 1 cup apple cider or white wine

3 cups cooked chicken, cut up

1/2 teaspoon fresh rosemary

1/2 teaspoon fresh thyme

1 tablespoon fresh parsley

1 teaspoon salt

1/4 teaspoon white pepper

2 cups cooked sliced carrots

2 cups cooked green peas

2 cups cooked pearl onions

2 cups sliced white mushrooms, sautéed

1 recipe pastry (see page 24)

1 egg yolk

1 tablespoon water

Preheat the oven to 425° F.

Melt the butter in a large saucepan over medium heat. Blend in the flour. Cook for several minutes. Add the milk and chicken broth. Cook until thickened, stirring constantly.

Add the chicken, rosemary, thyme, parsley, salt, and white pepper; mix well. Simmer, covered, for 5 to 10 minutes, stirring occasionally. Cool to room temperature. Add the carrots, peas, onions, and mushrooms; mix gently. Spoon the mixture into a 2 1/2-quart round baking dish.

Roll the pie pastry into a circle 1 inch larger than the top of the dish. Moisten the edge of the dish with water. Place the pastry on the top. Roll the edge of the pastry under and crimp to the edge of the dish. Brush with a mixture of the egg yolk and water.

Bake for 30 to 40 minutes or until the pastry is golden brown. Cut the pastry into wedges to serve and ladle the chicken mixture over the wedges.

MENU

A Holiday Celebration

SPICED BUTTERNUT SQUASH SOUP • LAMB WITH HERB-HAZELNUT CRUST • RASPBERRY BEET PUREE

GLAZED BABY CARROTS • BRUSSELS SPROUTS WITH PINE NUTS • MINTED ORZO WITH CURRANTS • BRITANNIA SALAD

CRANBERRY JEWEL CAKE • CHOCOLATE SPICE GINGER BOYS AND GIRLS • 1966 CHATEAU LAFITE ROTHSCHILD

Left overleaf, *A Holiday Celebration at the New York Junior League Headquarters,
the historic Astor townhouse on Manhattan's Upper East Side.*

Above, *Britannia Salad, a colorful combination of winter greens served with fresh apple slices and Stilton cheese.*

Left, *a bountiful sideboard displays Lamb with Herb-Hazelnut Crust.*

Below, *Spiced Butternut Squash Soup.*

Left, *Minted Orzo with Currants, sautéed Brussels Sprouts with Pine Nuts, Glazed Baby Carrots, and Raspberry Beet Purée.*

Above, *Cranberry Jewel Cake sparkles in candlelight.*

Above, *the holidays are not complete
without the magic
only children can bring.*

Below, *Chocolate Spice Ginger
Boys and Girls await Santa's visit.*

Serves Eight to Ten

Neuman & Bogdonoff has been a catering institution in Manhattan for years. This recipe from Steven Podel, at Neuman & Bogdonoff, goes well served over rice or rice and beans. Flour tortillas served on the side will make the most of the extra sauce.

Cut the chicken into 1-inch cubes. Rinse the cubes and pat dry. Combine the chicken with half the garlic, and the salt and pepper in a bowl; mix well.

Coat a heavy sauté pan with some of the oil. Heat the pan over medium heat until several drops of water will jump from the pan. Brown the chicken in several small batches in the heated pan; the chicken does not have to be completely cooked. Combine the browned chicken in a bowl and set aside; drain the pan, reserving the liquid in a bowl.

Brown the chorizo in the same manner in the sauté pan and set aside, reserving the cooking juices.

Sauté the onion in some of the remaining oil in the same sauté pan until translucent. Add the remaining garlic and the jalapeño peppers. Cook for 1 minute.

Add the tomatoes, vinegar, chili powder, cumin, red pepper sauce, and the reserved liquid from the chicken and chorizo. Cook, uncovered, over medium heat for 30 minutes.

Add the chicken and chorizo. Simmer for 10 minutes. Add the cilantro. Cook for 1 minute. Adjust the seasonings. Serve over steamed rice or with rice and beans.

4 pounds boneless chicken breasts

1 tablespoon chopped garlic

1/2 teaspoon salt

1/2 teaspoon freshly ground pepper

1 cup vegetable oil

1 pound Spanish chorizo, sliced 1/2 inch thick

1 medium onion, chopped

1–2 fresh jalapeño peppers, finely chopped

3 pounds plum tomatoes, peeled, seeded, and chopped, or 1 28-ounce can plum tomatoes

1/2 cup red wine vinegar

2 tablespoons chili powder

2 tablespoons cumin

1/2 teaspoon red pepper sauce

1/2 bunch fresh cilantro, coarsely chopped

BREAST OF GUINEA FOWL

This recipe comes to us from the magnificent restaurant Aureole, located on the East Side of Manhattan. Quail or chicken breasts can be substituted for the guinea fowl.

For the ragoût

1¼ cups dried green lentils

2 tablespoons olive oil

3 shallots, finely minced

¾ cup finely chopped carrot

1 clove of garlic, minced

1 bay leaf

2½ cups light chicken stock

1 tablespoon white vinegar

For the guinea fowl

6 breasts of guinea fowl with the wing joints, trimmed

12 fresh sage leaves

12 thin slices of pancetta
    salt and freshly cracked pepper to taste

2 tablespoons clarified unsalted butter

1 large white onion, coarsely chopped

¾ cup chicken stock

1 pound assorted wild mushrooms, coarsely chopped

1 tablespoon extra-virgin olive oil

1 tablespoon chopped parsley

TO MAKE THE RAGOUT:

Soak the lentils in water to cover in a bowl for 30 minutes; rinse well and drain.

Heat the olive oil in a saucepan and sauté the shallots for 1 minute. Add the carrot, garlic, and bay leaf. Sauté for 2 minutes longer. Add the lentils, stirring to coat well. Stir in the chicken stock and vinegar. Bring to a boil; reduce the heat. Simmer for about 15 minutes or until the lentils are tender but still whole; discard the bay leaf. Keep the lentils warm.

TO PREPARE THE GUINEA FOWL:

Preheat the oven to 375° F.

Place the guinea fowl pieces skin side up on a work surface. Arrange 2 sage leaves at an angle across each piece. Place 2 slices of pancetta on the sage leaves, overlapping the edges slightly. Tie with a fine twine to hold the pancetta in place. Season lightly with the salt and generously with pepper.

Heat the clarified butter in a large ovenproof nonstick skillet. Add the guinea fowl pieces bacon side down. Cook over medium heat for 8 to 10 minutes or until the bacon is rendered and the skin is brown. Remove the guinea fowl and drain the skillet.

Add the onion to the skillet. Sauté for 2 minutes. Place the guinea fowl skin side up on top of the onion. Bake for 8 to 10 minutes or until the guinea fowl is crisp and cooked through.

Remove the guinea fowl from the skillet and carefully remove the twine, leaving the pancetta in place; keep warm.

Add the chicken stock to the onion in the skillet. Bring to a boil. Strain the mixture and keep it warm.

TO PRESENT THE DISH:

Sauté the mushrooms in the olive oil in a sauté pan for 3 to 4 minutes. Add the parsley and adjust the seasoning.

Place 1 piece of guinea fowl on top of lentils which have been spooned onto each plate. Spoon mushrooms around the edge. Spoon pan juices over the top. Garnish with fresh sage leaves.

GINGER SOFTSHELL CRABS

Serves Four

Softshell crab fans will love this easy, light meal from Manhattan's Tavern on the Green restaurant. The pepper and onion compote makes this distinctive.

TO MAKE THE COMPOTE:

Sauté the onion, garlic, and ginger in the olive oil in a large sauté pan. Add the bell peppers, salt, and pepper. Simmer for 30 minutes.

TO PREPARE THE CRABS:

Soak the crabs in the milk in a bowl for 15 minutes; drain. Coat the crabs with a mixture of the flour and ginger, shaking off the excess flour mixture.

Melt the butter in the olive oil in a large heavy sauté pan. Sauté the crabs in 2 batches in the mixture until light brown on both sides.

Place 2 crabs on each heated serving plate. Top with the pepper compote and minced chives.

For the compote

1 medium onion, finely chopped

1 clove of garlic, minced

1 tablespoon minced fresh ginger

2 tablespoons olive oil

2 red bell peppers, seeded, chopped

2 yellow bell peppers, seeded, chopped

salt and freshly ground pepper to taste

For the crabs

8 softshell crabs

1½ cups milk

1½ cups flour

2 tablespoons ground ginger

3 tablespoons unsalted butter

2 tablespoons olive oil

2 tablespoons minced chives

CRISP SCALLOP AND SALMON CAKES

Serves Eight

Café des Artistes is an elegant, romantic, and long-time favorite restaurant located on Manhattan's West Side. At the Café, these are served as a warm luncheon dish with farmhouse potatoes and tomato-basil sauce. They are also delicious chilled, sliced, and served with a green salad.

1 cup chopped onion

1 tablespoon plus ½ cup unsalted butter, softened

1 cup white wine

12 ounces fresh salmon

4 ounces bay scallops

1 whole jalapeño pepper, seeded (optional)

1 large egg

1 tablespoon fresh lemon juice

1 tablespoon cognac

salt and freshly ground white pepper to taste

1 cup heavy cream

¼ cup chopped fresh dill

2 cups bread crumbs

¼ cup vegetable oil

Sauté the onion in 1 tablespoon butter in a sauté pan until tender. Add the wine. Cook until the liquid has completely evaporated.

Purée 4 ounces of the salmon, the scallops, and jalapeño pepper in a food processor. Add the egg, lemon juice, and cognac; process until smooth. Chill in the refrigerator.

Cream the remaining ½ cup butter with the salt and white pepper in a bowl. Add the seafood purée; mix well. Add the cream. Mix at low speed just until blended.

Chop the remaining 8 ounces salmon. Add to the puréed mixture with the sautéed onion and dill; mix well. Correct the seasoning if necessary. Chill until time to cook.

Shape the chilled mixture into 8 patties; coat with the bread crumbs. Fry in 2 batches in the heated oil in a heavy nonstick sauté pan over medium heat until golden brown on 1 side. Turn the patties over and reduce the heat slightly. Cook, covered, until cooked through.

Wollman Rink, near the southern end of Central Park, is a popular spot for skaters of all ages.

SALMON WITH WOVEN PASTRY CRUST

Serves Ten

Spinach and leeks nestled under the salmon provide wonderful flavor and beauty.

1 clove of garlic, crushed

1 large shallot, finely chopped

2 tablespoons Pernod

2 tablespoons unsalted butter

1 cup cooked chopped
   spinach, drained

1 large leek, julienned

1 tablespoon fresh lemon juice

2 sheets puff pastry

1 egg yolk, beaten

1 3- to 4-pound salmon fillet

Preheat the oven to 375° F.

Sauté the garlic, shallot, and Pernod in butter in a medium sauté pan for 1 minute. Add the spinach and leeks. Sauté for 1 minute. Stir in the lemon juice. Set aside to cool.

Spread 1 sheet of the puff pastry on a work surface. Brush the pastry with egg yolk. Spread the spinach mixture evenly down the center of the pastry. Place the salmon fillet on the spinach.

Brush the remaining sheet of pastry with the egg yolk. Cut into ¾-inch wide strips.

Place 1 strip of the pastry diagonally across the fish with the egg side down. Add strips parallel to the first strip and ¾ inch apart. Repeat the process with strips in the opposite direction. Crimp the edges to the bottom pastry with a fork. Trim away the excess pastry, leaving a 1-inch border.

Place on a baking sheet. Chill until time to bake.

Bake for 15 to 20 minutes or until the pastry is puffed and golden brown.

It's Christmas time in the city! A huge snowflake floats above Fifth Avenue at 57th Street.

At right, a wonderful way to explore Central Park on a warm winter day: a leisurely drive by hansom carriage.

SCAMPI STYLE LOBSTER TAILS

Serves Four to Six

Orzo provides a new addition to this quick but elegant entrée.

Cook the orzo using the package directions; keep warm.

Arrange the lobster in a single layer in a baking dish.

Melt the butter in a sauté pan over low heat. Stir in the worcestershire sauce, white wine, garlic, and lemon juice.

Pour the sauce over the lobster. Preheat the broiler. Broil the lobster for 3 minutes.

Turn the lobster over; sprinkle with the parsley. Broil for 3 minutes longer.

Spoon the lobster and the sauce over the orzo; sprinkle with the Parmesan cheese.

Variation Try substituting jumbo shrimp for the lobster tails and serve over rice or linguine.

1½ cups orzo

4 lobster tails

¾ cup unsalted butter

2 teaspoons worcestershire sauce

¼ cup dry white wine

1 large clove of garlic, minced

2 tablespoons fresh lemon juice

chopped fresh parsley

grated Parmesan cheese to taste

MAINE DAY-BOAT LOBSTER

Bouley, one of Manhattan's most acclaimed restaurants, shares this exciting entrée to try at home.

For the lobster

6 1¼-pound live Maine lobsters

flavorings per method

For the Tahitian vanilla sauce

1 Tahitian vanilla bean

½ cup sugar syrup

¾ cup sparkling cider

½ cup dark rum

¼ cup sherry wine vinegar

For the fricassée

1 stalk broccoli, florets and sliced stems

1 bunch baby carrots, cut into halves

1 bunch baby turnips, cut into halves

tips of 8 ounces asparagus

4 ounces French beans

4 ounces Roma beans

1 cup shell sugar snap peas or sweet peas

salt and freshly ground pepper to taste

chopped tarragon

Tahitian vanilla sauce

For the presentation

port wine paprika sauce (see page 105)

carrot sauce (see page 105)

pea sauce (see page 105)

TO PREPARE THE LOBSTER:

Remove the tail and claws from the body of the lobster. Cook them separately since they have different cooking times, and then you also have the "body" of the lobster to make into a lobster bisque or to make into a sauce. Put a large pot of water on to boil. Season the water with an onion cut in half, a stalk of celery, a small leek, or some fennel and a bay leaf. Cook the tails about 1½ minutes and the claws about 3 minutes. Make sure that the water continues to boil as the lobster parts are cooking. Be careful not to overcook the lobster since it will be reheated and "cooked" again. When the lobster is cool, remove the shells and set aside. Try to keep the claws intact when you remove them from the shell. Clean the tail by removing the intestine running along the bottom. The cooking liquid can be reduced and used as a "fish stock" in the sauce.

TO MAKE THE TAHITIAN VANILLA SAUCE:

Split the vanilla bean and scrape out the seeds. Combine the pod with the sugar syrup, sparkling cider, dark rum, and sherry wine vinegar in a small saucepan. Cook until the liquid is reduced by half. Keep warm in a *bain marie.*

TO MAKE THE FRICASSEE:

Blanch the broccoli, carrots, turnips, asparagus, and beans separately in a saucepan.

Layer the peas and blanched vegetables in a saucepan, sprinkling the layers with the salt, pepper, and chopped tarragon and spreading with the Tahitian vanilla sauce. Cook until the fricassée is heated through and the peas are tender.

TO ASSEMBLE THE DISH:

Place the fricassée on a serving plate. Arrange the heated lobster over the vegetables. Spoon some of the port wine paprika sauce over the lobster. Spoon the carrot sauce around one side of the plate; spoon the pea sauce around the other side. Serve immediately.

MAINE DAY-BOAT LOBSTER SAUCES

Serves Six

Th…*hese colorful sauces from Bouley can also be used to enhance other seafood presentations.*

TO MAKE THE CARROT SAUCE:

Simmer the carrot juice in a saucepan until reduced by 3/4. Add the caraway seeds. Simmer for several minutes. Whisk in enough butter over partial heat to cause the sauce to emulsify. Strain the sauce and keep warm in a *bain marie*.

TO MAKE THE PEA SAUCE:

Combine the peas, herbs, salt and pepper, and a small amount of the reduced lobster cooking liquid in a saucepan. Simmer just until the peas are tender. Adjust the seasonings and add the lemon juice. Keep the sauce warm in a *bain marie*.

TO MAKE THE PORT WINE PAPRIKA SAUCE:

Make a "mirepoix" and cook in butter in a heavy-bottomed pot until soft, stirring occasionally with a wooden spoon. Season with salt and pepper and sprinkle with paprika. Add the big soup spoon of tomato paste, 1 cup of fresh tomato and 1 cup of canned plum tomato and continue cooking. Add the white wine and let reduce. Chop the lobster "bodies" with a heavy knife or cleaver and sauté them in a little olive oil until they turn red and deglaze with cognac. Add to the pot and continue cooking for a few minutes. Meanwhile reduce some red wine and port in a small sauce pot by half. Make a paste with 1 teaspoon of flour and 1 teaspoon of butter. Add some of the lobster cooking water to cover the mirepoix and "bodies." Bring to a boil.

Skim and add the reduced wine, the flour/butter paste (to help thicken the sauce) and the fresh herbs.

Cook for 25 to 30 minutes, skimming as necessary. Strain the sauce and keep it warm in a *bain marie*.

For the carrot sauce

juice of 2 pounds carrots
pinch of caraway seeds
unsalted butter

For the pea sauce

1/2 cup fresh peas
chives, tarragon, and chervil or other fresh herbs
salt and freshly ground pepper to taste
reduced lobster cooking liquid
several drops of lemon juice

For the port wine paprika sauce

"mirepoix" of diced onion, shallot, carrot, celery, fennel, and leek
unsalted butter
salt, freshly ground pepper, and paprika to taste
1 large soup spoon tomato paste
1 cup chopped fresh tomato
1 cup canned plum tomato
a small amount of white wine
lobster shells
olive oil
cognac, red wine, and port wine to taste
1 teaspoon flour
1 teaspoon unsalted butter
reduced lobster cooking liquid
thyme, tarragon, or other fresh herbs

GRILLED SOUTHWESTERN TUNA

Summer barbecue delight. The tomato, black bean, and corn salsa makes this exceptional.

For the salsa

3 16-ounce cans black beans

1½ cups fresh or frozen corn, cooked

1½ cups chopped seeded tomatoes

⅓ cup finely chopped yellow onion

4–5 scallions, chopped

⅓ cup chopped cilantro leaves

½ cup extra-virgin olive oil

½ cup fresh lemon juice

1 tablespoon fresh lime juice

salt and freshly ground pepper to taste

⅓ cup mild picante sauce

1 teaspoon minced jalapeño pepper

For the tuna

6 yellowfin tuna steaks

¼ cup olive oil

¼ cup fresh lemon juice

3 tablespoons chili powder

3 tablespoons paprika

2 teaspoons ground cumin

2 tablespoons garlic powder

1 teaspoon cayenne pepper

1 teaspoon red pepper

1 teaspoon freshly ground black pepper

1 teaspoon salt

1 teaspoon oregano

K. Paul's blackened redfish seasoning to taste

1 bunch cilantro

TO MAKE THE SALSA:

Drain the beans and rinse the beans in a colander. Combine the beans with the corn, tomatoes, onion, scallions, and chopped cilantro in a bowl.

Whisk the olive oil, lemon juice, lime juice, salt, and pepper together in a small bowl. Add to the bean mixture; toss to mix well. Add the picante sauce and jalapeño pepper gradually until the mixture is as highly seasoned as desired. Chill until serving time. Serve chilled or at room temperature.

TO PREPARE THE TUNA:

Rinse the tuna and pat dry. Arrange in a glass baking dish in a single layer. Drizzle with the olive oil and lemon juice.

Combine the chili powder, paprika, cumin, garlic powder, cayenne pepper, red pepper, black pepper, salt, oregano, and blackened redfish seasoning in a ziplock bag. Shake until blended. Sprinkle the seasonings generously on both sides of the steaks.

Preheat the grill.

Let the tuna steaks stand, covered, at room temperature for 20 minutes. Place the steaks in a fish basket. Grill 4 to 6 inches from hot coals for 8 to 10 minutes or until the tuna flakes easily, turning once.

Place a mound of the salsa (see above) on each plate. Lay the tuna over the top. Garnish with cilantro sprigs.

Note If using fresh corn, cook the corn in boiling water in a saucepan for about 4 minutes; drain and cool. Better if it is made the day before and chilled to blend the flavors. If grilling inside, grill the tuna in 2 tablespoons olive oil over high heat for 3 to 4 minutes per side or until the steaks flake easily.

Variation Serve the salsa as a salad with grilled meat.

SZECHUAN SPICED SHRIMP

Served over brown rice, this makes a very healthy and easy dinner.

TO PREPARE THE SHRIMP:

Rinse the shrimp and pat dry; cut into halves lengthwise. Combine the Chinese wine, soy sauce, flour, cornstarch, egg, and baking soda in a bowl. Dip the shrimp in the mixture.

Heat the peanut oil in a wok over medium heat to 375° F. Stir-fry the shrimp in 2 batches for 10 seconds or until the shrimp turn light pink; drain. Transfer the shrimp to a bowl.

TO MAKE THE SAUCE:

Discard all but 2 tablespoons of the peanut oil. Heat the remaining peanut oil. Stir in the ginger root, garlic, scallions, and chili peppers. Cook until light brown, stirring constantly.

Stir in the sugar, soy sauce, sherry, white vinegar, and water. Cook until the mixture bubbles, stirring constantly.

Return the shrimp to the wok. Stir-fry for several seconds. Swirl in the sesame seed oil.

Remove the shrimp to a platter. Serve with steamed rice.

Note Having all the ingredients prepared for use before beginning is a necessity. The cooking process is so fast-moving that there is no time to work on preparation between steps.

For the shrimp

1 pound peeled deveined shrimp

1 teaspoon Chinese rice wine or pale dry sherry

1 teaspoon soy sauce

2 tablespoons flour

1 tablespoon cornstarch

1 egg, slightly beaten

1/4 teaspoon baking soda

2 cups peanut oil

For the sauce

1 teaspoon finely chopped ginger root

2 teaspoons minced garlic

2 scallions, finely chopped

2–3 dried chili peppers, chopped

1–3 tablespoons sugar

5 teaspoons black soy sauce

3 tablespoons pale dry sherry

1 teaspoon white vinegar

1 tablespoon water

1 teaspoon sesame seed oil

PESCE SPADA ALL GIUDIA

Serves Two

This delicious recipe for swordfish (it translates, swordfish steak Roman Jewish style) comes to us from a tiny family-run restaurant on the Upper East Side of Manhattan, Erminia.

2 4- to 6-ounce swordfish
  steaks
¼ cup flour
1–2 tablespoons olive oil
2 tablespoons unsalted butter
½ white onion, thinly sliced
2 teaspoons pine nuts
2 teaspoons golden raisins
1 bay leaf
  salt and freshly ground
  pepper to taste
⅓ cup white wine
4 teaspoons white wine vinegar
¼ cup fish stock
1 teaspoon chopped parsley
4–6 basil leaves

*Santa Claus shares his list with
two young elves in this recent
reenactment of the classic
Miracle on 34th Street.*

Coat the swordfish steaks with the flour. Sauté the steaks in the olive oil in an enamel sauté pan over medium heat until golden brown on both sides. Remove the swordfish to a plate; drain and wipe the sauté pan.

Melt the butter in the sauté pan over medium heat. Add the steaks, onion, pine nuts, raisins, bay leaf, salt, and pepper. Sauté for 2 to 3 minutes.

Add the wine and vinegar. Cook until the liquid is reduced by half. Add the fish stock. Cook for several minutes longer.

Remove the fish to a serving plate. Cook the stock until reduced to the desired consistency. Add the parsley and basil leaves; discard the bay leaf. Spoon over the fish and serve immediately.

MEDITERRANEAN SNAPPER PAPILLOTE

Serves Four

A dramatic presentation, the steaming packages may be opened at the table.

Preheat the oven to 400° F.

Prepare the parchment paper by cutting each sheet into a large heart shape. Set aside on a sheet pan.

Combine the onions, water, and salt in a stockpot. Boil for 4 minutes. Drain, reserving the onions and the liquid. Spread onions evenly among the four parchment hearts.

Bring the reserved liquid to a boil in the stockpot. Add the potatoes. Simmer for 5 minutes; drain. Layer the potatoes over the onions. Top with the sliced tomatoes. Sprinkle with the garlic; season with the salt and pepper.

Season the fillets with the salt and pepper. Place on top of the layered vegetables.

Pour the white wine and clam juice over the layers. Sprinkle with the thyme and rosemary. Place 1 lemon slice on each fillet. Drizzle with the olive oil.

Seal each parchment package by folding the paper over to cover the fish. Tuck edges in and roll to seal.

Bake for 15 minutes. Serve immediately.

Variation Black bass may be substituted for the red snapper.

4 sheets parchment paper

2 medium onions, thinly sliced

3 quarts water

  salt to taste

3 yellow gold potatoes, peeled, cut into halves lengthwise, thinly sliced

4 tomatoes, thinly sliced

2 cloves of garlic, chopped

  freshly ground pepper to taste

4 6-ounce red snapper fillets

1/2 cup dry white wine

1 12-ounce bottle of clam juice

1 teaspoon thyme

1 teaspoon rosemary

4 thin lemon slices

1/4 cup extra-virgin olive oil

ADDITIONS

SANDWICHES
BREAKFAST SWEETS
SIDE DISHES
SALADS

The perfect evening bag...the exceptional pair of earrings...the one-of-a-kind belt...every woman knows that accessories make the outfit. Talented is the chef who likewise envisions precisely what additions really make a meal, not just fill the plate. Vegetable dishes, potatoes, and salads should do more than complement an entrée. They will, with an imaginative eye to color, texture, and flavor, ultimately enhance the dining experience. Just as a fashion-conscious woman will adore experimenting with new accessories, so too will an enthusiastic chef delight in the fantastic fare included in this side-dish chapter.

Daytime—whether breakfast, lunch, or tea, is the best time to experiment with the delights of the recipes on the following pages. A formal occasion, such as *Tea in the Garden*, menu this page, calls for a delicate selection of tea sandwiches and, of course, an arrangement of sweets. Add a setting worthy of this fabulous fare—such as the serene garden at New York Junior League Headquarters—and you have the formula for New York entertainment at its most gracious.

Casual—are the recipes suggested for a dramatically different kind of afternoon, *Picnic in the Park*, menu on page 134. For true New Yorkers, there is only one park in the world. Begun in 1856, Central Park was classically created by Olmstead and Vaux. Today, the city's own backyard is for many New Yorkers, the only possible oasis. For Manhattan's children, it is a dream come true, and for those seeking casual al fresco dining, it provides an ever-changing array of memorable settings. A crisp day in autumn, which comes as respite to energize a summer-sated city, is a wonderful time to be outdoors and enjoy a luncheon picnic. Add close friends, smiling children, autumn fresh flowers, and you will have created a memory to treasure forever.

The additions in this chapter range from tea sandwiches to vegetable soufflés—from Lemon Yogurt Muffins to Love Apples with Herbs. They constitute a kaleidoscope of accompaniments that will ensure something for everyone—experiment with combinations and revel in sensational results.

MENU
Tea in the Garden

SELECTION OF TEA SANDWICHES:

CHOPPED EGG AND WATERCRESS

SMOKED TURKEY AND RASPBERRY BUTTER

WESTPHALIAN HAM, FRESH PINEAPPLE
AND HONEY MUSTARD

GRAVLAX OF SALMON WITH DILL BUTTER

CUCUMBER ROUNDS WITH
CHIVE MAYONNAISE

CHERRY CURRANT SCONES WITH
CLOTTED CREAM AND FRESH BERRIES

AN ASSORTMENT OF SWEETS:

LEMON CURD TARTLETS

BROWNIE PETITS FOURS

BUTTER COOKIE SHORTBREADS

LINZER HEART COOKIES

ORANGE POPPY SEED BREAD

LADY LONDONBERRY TEA
BERINGER WHITE ZINFANDEL

Left overleaf, *afternoon tea in the garden of the New York Junior League Headquarters ... showered with gifts.*

Left above, *Moist Orange Poppy Seed Bread.*
Left below, *Lemon Curd Tartlets.*
Above and right, *Cherry Currant Scones with fresh berries and clotted cream.*

Right overleaf, clockwise from top, *full-blown garden roses in watercolor hues.*
Vintage lace, silver, and crystal grace the table. Linzer Heart Cookies.
A cherub guards the tea trimmings. A selection of Tea Sandwiches.
Antique grape shears ...a useful and elegant touch. Brownie Petits Fours.

Variable Servings

T ea sandwiches are an elegant presentation for an afternoon shower. Use a variety of breads, shapes and combinations. The possibilities are infinite.

TEA SANDWICHES...

Extra-thin bread, either white, wheat, or whole grain, makes dainty closed sandwiches. Slices of chewy substantial bread, like pumpernickel or cinnamon-raisin, make a good base for open-face sandwiches. Consider tartlets, cream puffs, or even baby muffins as alternatives to traditional sandwich breads.

Cut off the bread crusts with a sharp serrated knife and cut the bread into decorative shapes with a knife or cookie cutters. While assembling sandwiches, keep the bread covered with a damp paper towel or plastic wrap to prevent drying out.

Lightly butter one side of the bread and add the desired spread. Assemble the sandwich with the filling of your choice. Try some of these spreads.

Mayonnaise Variations To mayonnaise, add Dijon mustard, freshly chopped dill or grated lemon rind, or try any of the Dipping Sauces on page 29.

Butter Variations To softened butter, fold in mashed fresh raspberries, chopped chives, or cream honey and orange zest.

Cream Cheese Variations To softened cream cheese, add chopped dates or raisins, fresh strawberries, or chutney.

TEA TRIMMINGS...

Of course, milk and sugar, but try English amber sugar crystals or French raw sugar cubes, lemon slices studded with cloves, peppermint leaves, or crystallized ginger.

Sandwich Ideas...

Smoked Turkey with Raspberry Butter

Cucumber with Chive Mayonnaise

Gravlax of Salmon with Dill Butter

Chopped Egg and Watercress

Westphalian Ham, Fresh Pineapple, and Honey Mustard

Crumbled Bacon, Avocado, and Sprouts

Smoked Chicken with Orange Honey Butter

Date Nut Bread with Strawberry Cream Cheese

ORANGE POPPY SEED BREAD

T his old-fashioned favorite is made new with a hint of orange.

For the bread

3 cups flour

2½ cups sugar

1½ teaspoons salt

1½ teaspoons baking powder

3 eggs, beaten

1½ cups milk

1 cup plus 2 tablespoons vegetable oil

3 tablespoons poppy seeds

1½ teaspoons vanilla extract

1½ teaspoons almond extract

1½ teaspoons butter extract

For the glaze

¼ cup orange juice

¾ cup sugar

½ teaspoon vanilla extract

½ teaspoon almond extract

½ teaspoon vegetable oil

TO MAKE THE BREAD:

Preheat the oven to 325° F.

Combine the flour, sugar, salt, baking powder, eggs, milk, oil, poppy seeds, and flavorings in a bowl; mix well.

Spoon the batter into 4 greased and floured miniature loaf pans. Bake for 45 minutes.

TO MAKE THE GLAZE:

Combine the orange juice, sugar, flavorings, and oil in a saucepan; mix well.

Cook over low heat until the sugar dissolves, stirring constantly.

Pierce the hot bread all over with a fork. Pour the glaze over the bread.

Note Good for brunch, at tea time, or as a dessert with ice cream, this bread is easy to make and freezes well.

Variation May bake the bread in 2 greased and floured 5-by-9-inch loaf pans. Bake for an hour or until the loaves test done.

BANANA MACADAMIA WAFFLES

Serves Fifteen

This unusual waffle recipe is a popular brunch entrée at the Stanhope Hotel and is wonderful.

Combine the flour and egg yolks in a mixer bowl. Add the milk gradually, beating constantly until smooth.

Stir in the butter, bananas, and half the nuts. Fold in the egg whites; the batter will be thick and frothy.

Cook in a waffle iron using the manufacturer's directions. Top with the remaining nuts, confectioners' sugar, and berries.

3 cups malted waffle flour

4 egg yolks, beaten

2 1/2 cups milk

3 ounces melted unsalted butter

2 very ripe bananas, mashed

1 cup crushed roasted macadamia nuts

4 egg whites, stiffly beaten

confectioners' sugar

fresh seasonal berries

CHERRY CURRANT SCONES

Serves Eight

Scones are traditional Scottish breakfast or tea fare. The word scone originates from the "Stone of Destiny" where Scottish kings were once crowned.

Preheat the oven to 425° F.

Combine the flour, 3 tablespoons sugar, baking powder, baking soda, and salt in a bowl. Cut in the butter until the mixture is crumbly. Add the buttermilk and currants; mix lightly with a fork to form a soft dough.

Knead the dough gently 5 or 6 times on a lightly floured surface. Roll 1/4 inch thick. Cut into sixteen 3-inch circles.

Place 8 of the circles on a greased baking sheet. Spoon 1 teaspoon of the jam into the center of each circle. Moisten the edges with water; top with the remaining circles, pressing the edges to seal. Sprinkle with the remaining 1 tablespoon sugar.

Bake for 15 to 18 minutes or until the scones are golden brown. Serve warm.

4 cups flour

4 tablespoons sugar

1 tablespoon baking powder

1/2 teaspoon baking soda

1/2 teaspoon salt

2/3 cup unsalted butter or margarine, softened

1 1/3 cups buttermilk

1/2 cup currants

8 teaspoons cherry preserves

LEMON YOGURT MUFFINS

Serve with coffee or tea, morning or afternoon.

For the muffins

2 cups flour

1 teaspoon baking powder

1 teaspoon baking soda

1/4 teaspoon salt

1/4 cup sugar

2 tablespoons honey

2 eggs

1 1/4 cups nonfat yogurt

1/4 cup unsalted butter

1 tablespoon finely grated lemon zest

confectioners' sugar for dusting

For the lemon syrup

1/3 cup lemon juice

1/3 cup sugar

3 tablespoons water

TO MAKE THE MUFFINS:

Preheat the oven to 350° F.

Mix the flour, baking powder, baking soda, and salt together; set aside.

Combine the sugar, honey, eggs, yogurt, butter, and lemon rind in a mixer bowl; mix well. Add the flour mixture; mix until moistened.

Spoon the batter into 6 large or 9 medium greased muffin cups, filling 3/4 full. Bake for 15 to 20 minutes or until golden brown. Cool for 5 minutes.

TO MAKE THE LEMON SYRUP:

Bring the lemon juice, sugar, and water to a boil in a small saucepan. Boil for 1 minute.

Drizzle the syrup over the muffins. Dust with confectioners' sugar.

Variation Three egg whites may be substituted for the 2 whole eggs to reduce cholesterol.

At right, May in Manhattan ushers in the dogwood blossoms, not only in Central Park but also here in Gramercy Park and in many smaller "vestpocket" parks throughout the city.

ASPARAGUS AU CITRON

Serves Four

Atasty and zesty side dish for spring and summer entertaining.

1½ pounds fresh asparagus

2 tablespoons grated fresh lemon zest

2 teaspoons anchovy paste

2 tablespoons fresh lemon juice

shaved Parmesan cheese to taste

Snap off the tough ends of the asparagus; peel the stalks. Steam the stalks in a small amount of water in a saucepan until tender-crisp. Refresh in ice water and drain.

Combine the lemon zest, anchovy paste, and lemon juice in a bowl; mix well.

Place the asparagus in a serving bowl. Spoon the lemon rind relish over the asparagus; garnish lightly with the shaved Parmesan cheese.

Note For a spectacular presentation, tie beautiful bows around bundles of asparagus using scallions or leeks which have been softened in boiling water.

RASPBERRY BEET PUREE

Serves Six

Garnet red beets create a wonderful jewel-like purée.

2 pounds fresh beets, tops and root ends removed

2 tablespoons raspberry vinegar

½ cup unsalted butter

1 teaspoon fresh lemon juice

1 tablespoon sugar

½ teaspoon salt

freshly ground pepper to taste

Cook the beets in water to cover in a saucepan for 40 to 50 minutes or until very tender; remove from the heat.

Rinse the beets under cold water, slipping off and discarding the skins. Cut into pieces. Purée in batches with the vinegar, butter, lemon juice, and sugar in a food processor. Add the salt and pepper. Add additional sugar if desired. Reheat in a double boiler to serving temperature.

BRUSSELS SPROUTS WITH PINE NUTS

Serves Four

The Four Seasons restaurant shares with us this wonderful way to prepare Brussels sprouts.

Clean the Brussels sprouts and cut a ¼-inch deep cross into the bottom of each. Add to salted boiling water in a saucepan. Cook for 5 to 8 minutes or until tender. Cool immediately in cold water; drain.

Sauté the pancetta in the olive oil in a sauté pan to render drippings. Add the shallots. Cook until the shallots are tender and the pancetta is crisp.

Add the Brussels sprouts, nutmeg, and pepper. Cook for 5 minutes, stirring frequently. Spoon into a serving dish.

Heat the butter in a small sauté pan until brown. Add the pine nuts. Sauté until the pine nuts are golden brown. Sprinkle over the Brussels sprouts.

2 cups Brussels sprouts
kosher salt to taste

2 ounces pancetta, finely chopped

1 tablespoon olive oil

2 shallots, finely chopped
freshly grated nutmeg to taste
freshly ground pepper to taste

1 tablespoon lightly salted butter

2 tablespoons pine nuts, crushed

Irving Place, which extends south from Gramercy Park to East 14th Street, was named after the author, Washington Irving.

GLAZED BABY CARROTS

This unusual recipe for baby carrots from the Four Seasons restaurant is well worth trying.

2 pounds baby carrots, peeled, trimmed

2 tablespoons lightly salted butter

2 tablespoons honey

kosher salt to taste

freshly ground pepper to taste

3½ ounces ginger ale

The Metropolitan Museum of Art, extending along Fifth Avenue from 80th to 84th Streets, is a composite of buildings. The original structure, designed by Calvert Vaux and Jacob Wrey Mould and completed in 1880, was a Victorian Gothic building oriented toward Central Park. The monumental Beaux Arts facade on Fifth Avenue, done by Richard Morris Hunt in 1902, has hidden the multiple extensions made both before and after.

Sauté the carrots in the heated butter in a saucepan for 1 minute. Add the honey, salt, and pepper; toss to coat well. Stir in the ginger ale gently. Bring to a boil; reduce heat.

Simmer, covered, for 3 minutes. Simmer, uncovered, for 5 minutes or until the carrots are evenly glazed.

SESAME BROCCOLI

Serves Four to Six

An easy and flavorful way to serve broccoli.

Steam the broccoli over boiling water in a saucepan just until tender-crisp; drain and cool to room temperature.

Combine the soy sauce, honey, sesame seeds, sesame oil, and sake in a bowl; mix well. Combine with the broccoli in a serving dish. Serve immediately.

Note May be prepared ahead, but do not mix the sauce with the broccoli until serving time.

florets of 1 bunch fresh broccoli

3 tablespoons soy sauce

2 teaspoons honey

1/4 cup toasted sesame seeds

2 teaspoons sesame oil

1/4 cup sake

CARROT SOUFFLE

Serves Six

Makes a nice addition to Sunday brunch.

Steam the carrots in a steamer for 20 minutes or until tender; drain. Purée in a food processor. There should be about 2 cups of carrot purée. Add the butter, sugar, eggs, cinnamon, flour, baking powder, salt, and milk to the carrots in the food processor; process until smooth.

Preheat the oven to 350° F.

Lightly butter a 1 to 1 1/2-quart soufflé dish or casserole or spray with vegetable cooking spray. Spoon the carrot mixture into the prepared dish. Bake for 45 minutes or until set.

1 pound carrots, peeled, grated

1/2 cup unsalted butter, softened

1/2 cup sugar

3 eggs

1/4 teaspoon cinnamon

1 tablespoon flour

1 teaspoon baking powder

1 teaspoon salt

1 cup milk

GREEN BEANS WITH ORANGE SAUCE

Agreat way to dress up green beans—beautiful and delicious.

1¼ pounds green beans
2 teaspoons unsalted butter
1 teaspoon olive oil
¼ cup chopped scallions
1 clove of garlic, minced
½ cup fresh orange juice
¼ cup dry white wine
2 quarts salted water
1 tablespoon grated orange zest

Trim the green beans and cut into halves lengthwise.

Heat the butter and olive oil in a small saucepan over low heat. Add the scallions and garlic. Sauté for 3 to 4 minutes or until the scallions are tender. Add the orange juice and wine; increase the heat to high. Cook for 4 minutes or until the mixture is thick and syrupy, stirring frequently; set aside and keep warm.

Bring the water to a boil in a saucepan over high heat. Add the green beans. Cook for 4 to 5 minutes or until the green beans are tender-crisp. Drain the green beans and pat dry.

Place the green beans in a serving dish. Add the sauce; toss gently. Sprinkle with the orange zest. Serve immediately.

RASPBERRY GREEN BEANS

Simple yet sophisticated.

¾ pound green beans
2 tablespoons unsalted butter
1 tablespoon raspberry vinegar
1 tablespoon rice vinegar
½ cup slivered almonds

Blanch the green beans in boiling water in a saucepan for 2 to 3 minutes or until the beans are bright green; drain and pat dry.

Melt the butter in a sauté pan over medium-low heat. Stir in the raspberry and rice vinegars and the green beans. Cook for 2 minutes over medium heat. Add the almonds; toss lightly to mix. Serve immediately.

Note For a special touch, add a few fresh raspberries to each plate.

Haricots Verts in Plum Tomatoes

Serves Four

An elegant presentation for a special dinner party.

Slice off the top and bottom of each tomato. Remove the pulp with a spoon to create hollow cylinders; set aside.

Trim the stem ends of the green beans. Steam the green beans in a saucepan for 3 to 5 minutes or just until tender; do not overcook. Place 12 green beans, or as many as will fit, in each tomato; arrange the tomatoes on a serving plate.

Combine the olive oil, vinegar, mustard, salt, and pepper in a bowl or blender container; whisk or process until smooth. Drizzle 1 teaspoon of the vinaigrette over each tomato.

4 plum tomatoes

48 haricots verts or very thin green beans

3/4 cup olive oil

1/3 cup red wine vinegar

1 tablespoon Dijon mustard

salt and freshly ground pepper to taste

Sweet Corn Ragout

Serves Four

A favorite from the Edson Hill Manor in Stowe, Vermont.

Cut the kernels from the ears of corn. Peel, seed, and coarsely chop the tomatoes.

Sauté the corn, bell pepper, zucchini, and scallions in the butter in a large sauté pan over high heat for 3 minutes. Add the tomatoes. Sauté for 1 minute.

Sprinkle with the thyme, parsley, salt, and pepper. Stir in the red pepper sauce and chicken stock. Cook for 1 minute longer. Spoon into a serving bowl.

Note Especially great with southwestern fare.

4 ears of sweet yellow corn, cooked

2 tomatoes

1 large red bell pepper, chopped

1 zucchini, finely chopped

4 scallions, thinly sliced

3 tablespoons unsalted butter

1 teaspoon chopped fresh thyme

2 tablespoons chopped fresh parsley

salt and freshly ground pepper to taste

3 drops of red pepper sauce

1/2 cup strong chicken stock

POTATOES WITH SHIITAKES AND BRIE

G*reat with grilled sausages and a mixed green salad.*

6 large new potatoes, scrubbed

1 teaspoon unsalted butter

8 ounces shiitake mushrooms

8 ounces Brie cheese

  salt and freshly ground
  pepper to taste

1 cup heavy cream

1 clove of garlic, minced

1 teaspoon thyme

3 tablespoons grated
  Parmesan cheese

1/4 cup fine dry bread crumbs

Left overleaf, Gramercy Park,
Manhattan's only private park,
is where residents of the
surrounding buildings receive
their own keys to the gate.

Slice the unpeeled potatoes 1/8 inch thick. Cover with cold water in a bowl. Let stand for 30 minutes, changing the water twice. Drain the slices and pat dry.

Preheat the oven to 425° F. Coat a 10-inch baking dish with the unsalted butter.

Remove the stems from the mushrooms and discard. Slice the caps thinly. Remove the rind from the cheese and cut into cubes (more easily done with firm, cold cheese).

Layer 1/3 of the potato slices in the buttered baking dish. Layer half the mushrooms and Brie, sprinkling the layers with the salt and pepper. Repeat the layers with the remaining potatoes, mushrooms, and Brie. Combine the cream, garlic, and thyme in a small bowl; mix well and pour over the layers, pressing the layers into the liquid.

Bake the casserole, covered with foil, for 30 minutes; remove the foil. Sprinkle with a mixture of the Parmesan cheese and bread crumbs. Bake, uncovered, for 30 minutes longer or until the top is golden brown and crusty.

PEARL ONION COMPOTE

Serves Four

A contemporary alternative to traditional holiday creamed onions.

Melt the butter in a sauté pan over medium heat. Add the onions and water. Cook for about 15 minutes or until the onions are caramelized. Stir in the raisins and pine nuts. Cook for 2 minutes.

Increase the heat to high. Stir in the brandy; remove from the heat. Ignite the brandy. Cook until the flames subside. Add the wine. Cook for 1 minute longer. Season with the salt and pepper.

Note To toast the pine nuts, cook in a small pan over low heat until brown. Be careful; they burn easily.

Variation This may be made with thawed frozen pearl onions, omitting the water.

6 tablespoons unsalted butter

1 cup fresh pearl onions, peeled

$1/2$ cup water

6 tablespoons raisins

2 tablespoons pine nuts, toasted

2 tablespoons brandy

2 tablespoons red wine

salt and freshly ground pepper to taste

SWISS STUFFED POTATOES

Serves Six

Try these with your next steak dinner instead of basic baked potatoes.

Preheat the oven to 350° F.

Bake the potatoes for 45 minutes to 1 hour or until the potatoes are tender. Cut the potatoes into halves and scoop the pulp into a bowl; reserve the shells.

Add the butter, chives, sour cream, nutmeg, salt, and pepper to the potatoes; mash until smooth. Spoon the mixture into the reserved shells; sprinkle with the cheese.

Place the stuffed potatoes on a baking sheet. Bake for 10 minutes or until golden brown.

Note Freezes well.

3 baking potatoes

$1^1/2$ tablespoons unsalted butter

1 tablespoon chopped chives

$1/2$ cup sour cream

nutmeg, salt, and freshly ground pepper to taste

3 tablespoons shredded Swiss cheese

SOUTHERN CORN PUDDING

Serves Six

Great with Herb-Roasted Chicken.

- 7–8 ears of corn, uncooked
- 3 eggs, slightly beaten
- 3 tablespoons melted unsalted butter
- 3 tablespoons sugar
- 1 cup plus 2 tablespoons milk, scalded
- 1½ teaspoons flour
- 1 teaspoon salt
- ⅛ teaspoon freshly ground pepper

Preheat the oven to 325° F.

Slice down each row of kernels on the ears of corn with a sharp knife; scrape the leftover pulp and juice from the cobs into a bowl with the back of the knife. Add the eggs, butter, sugar, milk, flour, salt, and pepper; mix well. Spoon into a greased baking dish.

Bake, uncovered, for 30 to 40 minutes or until the pudding is set.

Note Most of the pudding may be prepared in advance. Just add the eggs and milk at baking time.

POULTRY STUFFING WITH APRICOTS

Serves Ten

Made with Grand Marnier and dried apricots, this unusual recipe works with Cornish hens, ducklings or turkeys.

- 1 cup chopped dried apricots
- 1½ cups Grand Marnier
- poultry liver (optional)
- 2 cups coarsely chopped celery
- 1 large yellow onion, chopped
- 1 cup unsalted butter
- 1 pound bulk pork sausage
- 1 16-ounce package herb-seasoned stuffing mix
- 1 cup slivered almonds
- 2 cups chicken broth
- ½ teaspoon thyme
- salt and freshly ground pepper to taste

Bring the apricots to a boil in 1 cup of the Grand Marnier; remove from the heat and set aside.

Simmer the liver in water to cover in a small saucepan for 5 minutes. Cool and chop.

Sauté the celery and onion in ½ cup butter in a large sauté pan over medium heat for 10 minutes. Remove to a large bowl with a slotted spoon.

Cook the sausage in the drippings in the sauté pan, stirring until crumbly. Add the sausage, stuffing mix, apricots, and almonds to the sautéed vegetables in the bowl. Stir in the liver.

Melt the remaining ½ cup butter in the chicken broth in a small saucepan. Add to the stuffing mixture with the remaining ½ cup Grand Marnier; mix well. Season with the thyme, salt, and pepper.

Stuff into the poultry cavity and roast accordingly.

MENU
Picnic in the Park

**BLOODY MARY GAZPACHO RIMMED
WITH FRESH SHRIMP**

DISHEVILED EGGS

MINI PAN BAGNAS

PASTA NIÇOISE A LA GRECQUE

SWEET CORN RAGOUT

MADISON SQUARES

FRESH FRUIT SKEWERS

SELECTION OF SOFT DRINKS

Left overleaf, *harvest sunflowers
and an antique patchwork quilt
provide additional autumn
background for picnic fare in
Manhattan's Central Park.
Mini Pan Bagnas can be made
ahead and sliced at picnic time.*

Left, *Sweet Corn Ragoût,
appropriately and enticingly
presented in a wooden treucher.*

Above right, *cold poached shrimp
rim old mason jars filled
with Bloody Mary Gazpacho.
Nostalgic Coca-Cola bottles enhance
the mood. Disheviled Eggs
travel nicely to the picnic.*

Below left to right,
*Pasta Niçoise à la Grecque.
Harvest sunflowers.
Madison Squares with macadamia
nuts and do-ahead fruit skewers.*

Right overleaf, *majestic
Bethesda Fountain in Central Park
provides a magical backdrop for
a memorable meal.*

TOMATO TART

Serves Four to Six

E xcellent either as a main entrée for a vegetarian supper or as a side dish.

Preheat the oven to 350° F.

Bake the pie shell for 10 minutes. Cool for 5 to 10 minutes.

Spread the mustard in the bottom of the pie shell. Arrange the cheese in the prepared pie shell. Arrange the tomato slices in concentric circles over the cheese in an overlapping layer, beginning at the outer edge. Sprinkle the tart evenly with the garlic, basil, salt, and pepper. Drizzle with the olive oil.

Place the tart on a baking sheet. Bake for 40 minutes.

1 unbaked pie shell

2 tablespoons Dijon mustard

8 ounces mozzarella cheese, sliced 1/4 inch thick

4 medium tomatoes, sliced

1–2 cloves of garlic, finely chopped

2 tablespoons fresh chopped basil

salt and freshly ground pepper to taste

2 tablespoons olive oil

LOVE APPLES WITH HERBS

Serves Four to Six

C olorful and easy. Serve with grilled meats or fish.

Preheat the oven to 375° F.

Pour the olive oil into a 9-by-13-inch baking dish. Place the tomatoes in a single layer in the prepared dish, turning to coat well with the oil. Sprinkle with the herbs, sugar, salt, and pepper.

Bake, covered with foil, for 5 minutes. Bake, uncovered, for 10 minutes longer or just until the tomatoes are tender; do not overcook, as the tomatoes will split open.

2 tablespoons olive oil

1 pint red cherry tomatoes

1 pint yellow cherry tomatoes

2–4 tablespoons mixed fresh herbs, such as parsley, chives, tarragon, and dill

sprinkle of sugar

salt and freshly ground pepper to taste

SOUFFLE AU GRUYERE

A *classic. Serve as a first course or with a green salad for an elegant light meal.*

½ cup unsalted butter

½ cup flour

2¼ cups milk

½ teaspoon salt

    freshly ground pepper to taste

5 eggs, separated

1–1½ cups shredded Gruyère cheese

    additional salt to taste

Preheat the oven to 350° F.

Melt the butter in a saucepan. Add the flour alternately with the milk, stirring constantly and cooking until bubbly between each addition. Stir in the ½ teaspoon salt and pepper; remove the saucepan from the heat.

Beat the egg yolks. Stir a small amount of the hot sauce into the egg yolks; stir the egg yolks into the hot mixture. Stir in the cheese until melted.

Combine the egg whites with salt to taste in a mixer bowl; beat until stiff peaks form. Fold in the egg yolk mixture gently.

Spoon the mixture into a greased soufflé dish. Bake for 35 to 40 minutes or until the soufflé is set. Serve immediately.

SOHO BEEF SALAD

Serves Two

SoHo is the area of Manhattan south of Houston Street known for its artists' lofts and galleries. This salad's colors and flavors make it a work of art befitting its name.

TO MAKE THE DRESSING:

Combine the honey, soy sauce, rice wine vinegar, and tamari in a bowl. Add the oils very gradually, beating constantly with a wire whisk until blended.

TO MAKE THE SALAD:

Roll the chunks of goat cheese in the sesame seeds. Place on a microwave-safe dish. Microwave on High for 12 seconds or until the cheese is soft but retains its shape.

Combine the mesclun, julienned roast beef, new potatoes, and bacon in a bowl. Add the dressing, tossing to coat. Divide the salad evenly between two plates. Garnish with the chopped onion and avocado. Top with the warm goat cheese.

Note Serve this salad with pita bread split open, buttered, and sprinkled with white sesame seeds, then broiled until light brown. Black sesame seeds can be purchased in health food stores.

Variation Use grilled beef tenderloin or sirloin instead of the roast beef.

For the dressing

1 tablespoon honey

2 teaspoons light soy sauce

1/4 cup rice wine vinegar

1/4 cup tamari

1 tablespoon sesame oil

1 tablespoon chili oil

2 tablespoons vegetable oil

For the salad

2 1-ounce chunks goat cheese

1 tablespoon black sesame seeds

3 cups mesclun, rinsed, spun or patted dry

4 ounces rare roast beef, julienned

2 large new potatoes, cooked, thinly sliced

2 slices cooked bacon, crumbled

finely chopped Vidalia onion

sliced avocado

CURRIED CHICKEN SALAD

Serves Six

A *flavorful salad that may be garnished with fresh tropical fruits for a colorful entrée or spooned into miniature tartlet shells for a unique hors d'oeuvre.*

3 pounds chicken breasts
(about 4 cups chopped
cooked chicken)

2 tablespoons fresh lemon juice

1/2 cup each chopped red and
yellow bell pepper

1 bunch scallions with tops,
sliced

1 cup dried currants

1 cup sliced almonds

1/4 cup plain yogurt

1/4 cup mayonnaise

3 tablespoons chutney

3 tablespoons honey mustard

1 1/2 teaspoons curry powder

1/2 teaspoon ground cumin
salt and freshly ground
pepper to taste

*Left overleaf, Gramercy Park
is a cascade of color from
spring through autumn and is
distinguished by Greg Wyatt's
fanciful fountain with giraffes
dancing around the sun and
Edwin Quinn's statue of
Edwin Booth playing Hamlet.*

Combine the chicken, lemon juice, bell peppers, scallions, currants, and almonds in a large bowl; toss to mix well.

Whisk the yogurt and mayonnaise together in a small bowl. Whisk in the chutney and honey mustard; use the back of a spoon to crush any large pieces of the chutney. Add the curry powder, cumin, salt, and pepper; mix well.

Add the dressing to the chicken mixture; mix lightly. Chill the salad until serving time.

Serve on a bed of mixed greens.

Note For a smoother salad, pulse in a food processor to chop more finely.

Variation To serve as an hors d'oeuvre, spoon the more finely chopped salad into tartlet shells (see page 24).

WARM CASHEW CHICKEN SALAD

Serves Four

The combination of crunchy cashews and colorful tangy oranges makes this salad exceptional.

Toss the romaine lettuce, spinach, and mandarin oranges in a bowl. Rinse and pat dry the chicken breasts; cut into 1-inch pieces. Heat the vegetable oil in a large sauté pan over medium-high heat. Stir-fry the chicken in the hot oil for 5 to 7 minutes. Add the scallions and garlic; mix well. Cook for 1 minute, stirring constantly. Stir in a mixture of the soy sauce, honey, ginger, and water. Cook for 30 seconds, stirring constantly.

Spoon the chicken and the sauce over the lettuce mixture, tossing gently until combined; sprinkle with the cashews. Serve immediately.

Note Buy raw, unsalted cashews and gently toast on a cookie sheet in the oven at 300° F. Keep an eye on them; nuts burn quickly.

2 cups bite-sized pieces romaine lettuce

8 ounces spinach, shredded

1 11-ounce can mandarin oranges, drained

1¼ pounds boneless chicken breasts

3 tablespoons vegetable oil

3 tablespoons chopped scallions

1 clove of garlic, minced

3 tablespoons soy sauce

1 tablespoon honey

¼ teaspoon ground ginger

3 tablespoons water

¼ cup cashews

COS COB SALAD

Serves Six to Eight

A nouvelle version of the traditional Cobb Salad from the environs of Manhattan.

Tear the lettuce into bite-sized pieces. Place in a crystal bowl. Arrange the tomatoes, mozzarella cheese, avocados, crumbled bacon, scallops, and cheddar cheese in sections over the lettuce in the order listed. Serve with the vinaigrette.

Note The salad, undressed, may be made one day ahead, but the bacon will not be as crisp if made ahead, so save it until the last minute. Squeeze a lime over the avocado slices to keep the avocados from turning brown, or slice the avocados at the last minute.

1 head red leaf or Bibb lettuce

1 small head romaine lettuce

2 tomatoes, cut 1 inch thick

1 pound mozzarella cheese, shredded

2 avocados, cut 1 inch thick

1 pound bacon, cooked

1½ pounds bay scallops, cooked

4 cups shredded cheddar cheese

vinaigrette (see page 148)

FOIE GRAS SALAD

An elegant salad which can be served before or after your main course.

For the salad

12 ounces salad greens, including watercress, radicchio, spinach, endive, and chicory

2 tablespoons chopped fresh herbs, including parsley, chives, tarragon, and basil

2 plum tomatoes, thinly sliced

1 tablespoon unsalted butter

1 tablespoon olive oil

1 small red onion, sliced into thin rings

1 cup sliced mushrooms

For the dressing

3 tablespoons olive oil

2 tablespoons raspberry vinegar

1 teaspoon Dijon mustard

1 teaspoon sugar

salt and freshly ground pepper to taste

For the presentation

4 ounces *pâté de foie gras* with truffles, cut into 12 slices

TO MAKE THE SALAD:

Wash, dry, and tear the salad greens into pieces.

Combine the salad greens, fresh herbs, and tomatoes in a bowl; mix well.

Melt the butter with the olive oil in a sauté pan. Sauté the onion in the sauté pan until golden brown, stirring constantly. Add the mushrooms, tossing to coat. Add the sautéed onions and mushrooms to the salad green mixture; mix well. Reserve the pan juices in the sauté pan.

TO MAKE THE DRESSING:

Combine the olive oil, raspberry vinegar, Dijon mustard, and sugar in the same sauté pan; mix well. Cook over medium heat until heated through, stirring constantly. Season with the salt and pepper.

Pour the dressing over the salad green mixture, tossing to coat evenly. Divide the salad evenly among 4 salad plates. Top each salad with 3 slices of the *pâté de foie gras*.

Note Serve with warm sourdough baguettes.

*The Bethesda Fountain, in Central Park, was dedicated in 1873; the statue on top, **Angel of the Waters**, commemorates the 1842 opening of the Croton Aqueduct.*

CHELSEA CRAB MEAT SALAD

C helsea, a neighborhood in the low 20's on the West Side of Manhattan, boasts of interesting shops and restaurants of all types.

2 pounds fresh crab meat, shredded

5–6 tablespoons mayonnaise or plain nonfat yogurt

1 tablespoon coarse mustard

2 teaspoons curry powder

4 teaspoons cayenne pepper

salt and freshly ground black pepper to taste

2 tablespoons fresh lemon juice

1 cup chopped celery hearts

1 Vidalia onion, chopped

4 hard rolls

Combine the crab meat, mayonnaise, mustard, curry powder, and cayenne pepper in a bowl; mix well. Season with the salt and black pepper to taste. Sprinkle the lemon juice over the salad.

Stir in the chopped celery hearts and chopped Vidalia onion. Serve in the hard rolls.

Note It is important to use a Vidalia onion, which is mild and sweet, in order not to overpower the delicate taste of the crab meat.

Variation For lighter fare, substitute endive leaves for the rolls.

CAJUN SHRIMP REMOULADE SALAD

Serves Twelve

Start your meal with this tasty shrimp remoulade served on a bed of mixed greens.

TO PREPARE THE SHRIMP:

Place the shrimp in a stockpot filled with cold water. Stir in the Old Bay Seasoning, lemon slices, and bay leaves. Boil the shrimp for 2 to 3 minutes or until the shrimp turn pink. Drain, peel, and devein the shrimp; store in the refrigerator.

TO MAKE THE REMOULADE SAUCE:

Combine all of the ingredients in a bowl; mix well. Stir in the shrimp. Chill, covered, for several hours to overnight.

Serve on the mixed greens.

Note The remoulade sauce is best if prepared the day ahead to allow the flavors to marry and give the shrimp that fresh-from-the-bayou taste. Freezes well.

Variation Serve as an hors d'oeuvre by skewering the shrimp on colorful toothpicks and inserting into a head of cabbage. Trim the base of the cabbage to prevent it from wobbling.

For the shrimp

3 pounds medium-sized unpeeled shrimp

1/2 cup Old Bay Seasoning or shrimp boil

3 lemon slices

2 bay leaves

For the remoulade

1/4 cup apple cider vinegar

1/2 onion, thinly sliced

1 tablespoon worcestershire sauce

3/4 cup catsup

2 cups olive oil

1/2 cup spicy creole mustard

3 tablespoons fresh lemon juice

cayenne pepper to taste

1 teaspoon paprika

2 tablespoons freshly chopped parsley

1 teaspoon oregano

1 teaspoon red pepper sauce

1/2 cup horseradish, drained

For the presentation

mixed greens

BRITANNIA SALAD

This salad is especially wonderful for the holidays. Serve it with chunks of Stilton cheese and toasted baguette slices.

For the vinaigrette

¼ cup sherry vinegar

1 tablespoon Dijon mustard

salt and freshly ground pepper to taste

½ cup olive oil

2 Granny Smith apples, cored and cut into ⅛-inch slices

For the salad

1 small bulb of fennel

1 small head radicchio

1 medium head frisée or chicory

TO MAKE THE VINAIGRETTE:

Combine the vinegar, mustard, salt, and pepper in a bowl. Add the olive oil gradually, whisking until the mixture is smooth. Add the apple slices. Marinate in the refrigerator for up to 2 hours.

TO MAKE THE SALAD:

Cut the fennel into thin crescent shapes. Combine with the torn radicchio and frisée in a bowl; mix lightly. Chill until serving time.

Add the vinaigrette and apples at serving time; toss gently to mix.

Serves Eight

A wonderfully colorful salad to accompany any meal.

TO MAKE THE DRESSING:

Combine the olive oil and wine vinegar in a bowl. Beat with a whisk until blended.

TO MAKE THE SALAD:

Combine the tomatoes and mangos in a bowl; mix well. Add the dressing, tossing to coat. Arrange on a bed of watercress. Season with the salt and pepper; sprinkle with the chopped red onion. Garnish with the chopped basil if desired. Serve immediately.

Variation Substitute papayas for mangos and cilantro for basil.

For the dressing

3 tablespoons extra-virgin olive oil

2 tablespoons white wine vinegar

For the salad

8 medium tomatoes, cut into wedges

2 large mangos, chopped

2 bunches watercress

salt and freshly ground pepper to taste

1 tablespoon finely chopped red onion

chopped fresh basil (optional)

Pastas & Grains

Pastas
Grains
Savory Breads

$\mathscr{P}$astas and grains—topped with freshly made sauce or blended with a melange of ripe vegetables—are among the most versatile, most nutritious, and most satisfying dishes any chef can cook. Whether prepared as a main or side dish, whether served hot or cold, pasta and its related grains need only the adornment of a fresh salad to be complete.

After having mastered the simplest of sauces, the pasta lover is more than ready to try something new. The recipes in this chapter provide an infusion of unique combinations that will inspire even the most jaded cook. While Italy is the country most often associated with pasta, the recipes that follow have been enhanced by the flavors of China, France, Greece, Mexico, England and other countries not traditionally linked to pasta or grains. Add flowers, wine and music and presto! You have created a taste of Manhattan uniquely your own.

Home from work just minutes before your guests are arriving? If you have planned a *Pasta Kitchen Party*, then there is sure to be time to spare—the fare included on this menu can all be prepared in advance. Spaghetti Con Vongole e Carciofi, Pasta Cruda and Spinach Porcini Lasagna are all main course pasta dishes with sauces, like fine wine, which actually improve with time. Assemble all in the company of your guests and you have created an irresistibly casual evening—as comforting as the dishes themselves.

Few people can resist well-made pasta. Why not take advantage of this innate predilection for pasta and make it the focal point of your meal? If your goal is to dress up a chop or enhance a roast, sample one or more of the unusual rice and risotto recipes which follow. Jeweled Rice Salad or Wild Mushroom Risotto may be just the dish you are searching for. Look no further than what is ahead for the perfect pastas and grains!

MENU
Pasta Kitchen Party

TRICOLOR SALAD OF ARUGULA, RADICCHIO AND FRISEE WITH SHAVED PARMESAN

PASTA CRUDA

SPINACH AND PORCINI LASAGNA

SPAGHETTI CON VONGOLE E CARCIOFI

FOCCACCIA BREAD

TIRAMISU

VILLA ANTINORI BIANCO

MONSALLETTO BAROLO

ESPRESSO

Left overleaf, *Abbondanza! A do-ahead informal pasta feast.*

Above left, *Spaghetti Con Vongole e Carciofi combines artichokes with clams.*

Below left, *Spinach Porcini Lasagna served on candy-colored ceramics.*

Above, *leftover herbs and spices can flavor oils and vinegars.*
Blend different combinations to adorn salad greens.

Right overleaf, *Tiramisu, the perfect ending.*

SPAGHETTI CON VONGOLE E CARCIOFI

Serves Eight

From *Il Cantinori restaurant, a Greenwich Village highlight, this is an Italian favorite that is low in fat.*

Soak, wash, and clean the clams. Soak the artichoke hearts in 1 cup of water combined with the lemon juice.

Steam the clams in ½ cup of the white wine in a large stockpot over medium heat until clams open. Remove all but 12 to 16 clams from the shells. Reserve these whole clams in the shells for garnish.

Cook the pasta in a large pot of boiling water until *al dente*; drain.

Sauté the garlic in olive oil and the remaining ½ cup of white wine in a large sauté pan over medium heat.

Drain the artichokes; add to garlic mixture, cooking until tender. Add the clams; simmer for 5 minutes.

Add the cooked pasta to the sauté pan and toss. Add the red pepper flakes to taste. Sprinkle with the parsley.

3 dozen manilla clams (approximately 2 cups clams, shelled)

1 cup baby artichoke hearts, cut into quarters

1 cup water

2 tablespoons fresh lemon juice

1 cup white wine

2 pounds uncooked spaghetti

2 cloves of garlic

¼ cup olive oil

red pepper flakes to taste

½ cup coarsely chopped flat parsley

FARFALLE IN LIGHT HERB BROTH

Serves Four

Serve this colorful dish with a chilled white wine for a delightful summer dinner.

20 medium to large asparagus stalks

1 pound uncooked farfalle pasta

6 tablespoons cornstarch

1 14-ounce can chicken broth

1/2 teaspoon finely chopped garlic

1/4 cup virgin olive oil

4 ounces thinly sliced prosciutto

5 ounces sundried tomatoes in olive oil

2 tablespoons basil, sliced

2 tablespoons coarsely chopped parsley

1 tablespoon chopped fresh dill

freshly ground pepper to taste

grated Parmesan cheese to taste

Peel and trim 1 inch from the stems of the asparagus. Blanch in boiling water in a saucepan for 20 seconds; drain and cool. Slice diagonally into 1-inch pieces; set aside.

Cook the pasta in a large pot of boiling water until *al dente*; drain.

Blend the cornstarch with 2 ounces of the chicken broth in a small bowl. Add the remaining broth to a saucepan and bring to a boil. Whisk in the cornstarch mixture. Cook until thickened, stirring constantly; remove from the heat.

Sauté the garlic in the heated olive oil in a sauté pan. Add the prosciutto, tomatoes, asparagus, basil, parsley, dill, and pepper. Sauté for 30 seconds. Stir in the thickened chicken broth.

Bring to a simmer. Add the pasta. Simmer until heated through. Serve immediately; sprinkle with the cheese.

Note Farfalle is the Italian word for butterfly. It is often referred to as bowtie pasta.

FETTUCINI WITH POACHED LOBSTER

Serves Four to Six

From the shores of Nantucket to the streets of Manhattan, De Marco Restaurant shares with us this low-fat dish.

Cook the lobster in boiling water in a large stockpot for 8 to 10 minutes; drain and place in ice water. Remove the lobster meat from the shell and knuckles; cut the tail meat into halves lengthwise. Leave the claws intact. Chill the lobster in the refrigerator.

Combine the celery juice, white wine, and shallots in a saucepan. Cook until reduced by half; set aside.

Sauté the ginger, garlic, mushrooms, snow peas, and bell pepper in sesame oil in a sauté pan until tender. Add the celery broth mixture and lobster; mix well. Cook over low heat until heated through; season with the salt and pepper to taste. Keep the sauce warm.

Cook the fettucini in a large pot of boiling water until *al dente*; drain. Toss with the lobster mixture in a bowl. Spoon onto individual serving plates; garnish with the sesame seeds.

Note Celery juice may be purchased in health food stores. Use fresh or frozen lobster meat in this recipe if there is not time to shell the lobster. To toast sesame seeds, place evenly on cookie sheet and bake at 350° for a few minutes until lightly browned. Watch carefully so as not to burn.

2¼ pounds lobster

1 cup celery juice

¼ cup white wine

2 tablespoons chopped shallots

1 teaspoon chopped fresh ginger root

1 teaspoon minced garlic

1 cup julienned shiitake mushrooms

¼ cup julienned snow peas

¼ cup juilienned red bell pepper

1 teaspoon sesame oil

salt and freshly ground pepper to taste

1 pound uncooked fettucini

toasted sesame seeds

TAGLIATELLE WITH GOAT CHEESE

A sparagus, shrimp, and shiitake mushrooms make this pasta extra special.

1 pound fresh asparagus

salt to taste

8 ounces shiitake mushrooms, sliced, stems removed

1/2 cup minced shallots

2 tablespoons unsalted butter

1/2 cup dry white wine

1/2 cup chicken broth

1/2 cup heavy cream

6 ounces mild goat cheese, crumbled

12 ounces cooked shrimp, coarsely chopped

1/4 cup minced fresh chives

freshly ground pepper to taste

1 pound uncooked tagliatelle or fettucini

Trim the asparagus and peel the stems. Slice the spears on the bias into 1/2-inch pieces. Cook with the salt to taste in boiling water to cover in a saucepan for 2 to 3 minutes or just until tender; drain. Refresh under cold water; drain well.

Cook the mushrooms and shallots in butter in a heavy sauté pan over low heat until tender, stirring constantly. Add the wine. Simmer until the wine is reduced by half.

Add the chicken broth, cream, and cheese. Cook over low heat until the cheese melts, stirring to mix well. Stir in the shrimp, asparagus, chives, salt, and pepper. Keep the sauce warm.

Cook the tagliatelle in a large pot of boiling water until *al dente*; drain. Toss with the sauce in a large bowl. Serve immediately.

Note When choosing a goat cheese, look for a mild, creamy version such as Montrachet.

Variation May serve as an appetizer for six to eight.

At right, Little Italy, located on the Lower East Side from Houston to Canal Streets, and Lafayette Street to the Bowery, hosts some of Manhattan's best old-world Italian restaurants.

HEAVENLY PASTA

A *simple dish for a busy cook. Combine the ingredients before leaving for work and dinner will be virtually ready when you return!*

4 pounds fresh tomatoes, chopped

½ cup chopped sundried tomatoes

½ bunch fresh spinach, torn

8 ounces Brie cheese, rind removed, diced

2 tablespoons basil

1 tablespoon parsley

2 tablespoons minced garlic

½ cup extra-virgin olive oil

1 teaspoon freshly ground pepper

1 pound uncooked linguine

grated Parmesan cheese to taste

Combine the fresh tomatoes, sundried tomatoes, spinach, Brie cheese, basil, parsley, garlic, olive oil, and pepper in a bowl; mix well. Let stand for 4 to 12 hours.

Cook the pasta in a large pot of boiling water until *al dente*; drain. Add the marinated mixture; toss to mix well. Serve with the Parmesan cheese.

Serves Eight to Ten

G*reat to make ahead for a party.*

TO MAKE THE MUSHROOM CREAM SAUCE:

Sauté the mushrooms in ¼ cup of the butter in a sauté pan; set aside. Melt the remaining ¼ cup butter in a saucepan. Whisk in the flour. Cook for several seconds. Whisk in the cream gradually. Add the salt and pepper. Cook until thickened, stirring constantly. Fold in the sautéed mushrooms. Cook for 1 minute longer.

TO MAKE THE LASAGNA:

Preheat the oven to 350° F.

Cook the lasagna noodles in a large pot of boiling water using package directions; drain.

Sauté the onion in the butter in a large sauté pan until tender. Stir in the cream cheese, cottage cheese, egg, salt, pepper, and basil.

Combine the mushroom cream sauce, wine, shrimp, and crab meat in a bowl; mix well.

Layer the noodles, the cottage cheese mixture, and the seafood mixture ⅓ at a time in a large greased baking dish. Sprinkle with the Parmesan cheese.

Bake, covered, for 45 minutes. Top with the cheddar cheese and paprika. Bake for 2 to 3 minutes longer. Let the lasagna stand for 15 minutes before serving.

Note This recipe may be prepared ahead of time and frozen.

For the mushroom cream sauce

2 cups sliced fresh mushrooms
½ cup unsalted butter
¼ cup flour
2 cups cream
   salt and freshly ground pepper to taste

For the lasagna

1 pound uncooked lasagna noodles
1 cup chopped onion
2 tablespoons unsalted butter
8 ounces cream cheese
1½ cups cottage cheese
1 egg, beaten
½ teaspoon salt
½ teaspoon freshly ground pepper
2–3 teaspoons dried basil
   mushroom cream sauce
½ cup dry white wine
2 pounds fresh shrimp, cooked, peeled
8 ounces frozen crab meat, thawed
¼ cup grated Parmesan cheese
½ cup shredded sharp cheddar cheese
   dash of paprika

LASAGNA WITH ROASTED ASPARAGUS

Serves Four

Made with goat cheese and roasted asparagus, this sophisticated 1990's version of lasagna is great at dinner parties or, cut into smaller pieces, served as an appetizer.

2 pounds fresh asparagus

2–3 tablespoons olive oil

1 pound no-boil lasagna noodles

1 tablespoon fresh lemon juice

1 teaspoon salt

2 tablespoons unsalted butter

¼ cup flour

1½ cups chicken broth

1 3½-ounce package herbed Montrachet goat cheese with chives

⅔ cup grated Parmesan cheese

freshly ground pepper to taste

1 package garlic and herb cheese such as Boursin or Alouette

2 tablespoons milk

Preheat the oven to 500° F.

Break off about 1 inch from the ends of the asparagus stems; peel the stems and trim the ends. Cut off the tips and set aside. Coat the asparagus stalks with olive oil; place on a baking sheet. Roast for about 7 or 8 minutes or until just tender. Cut the stalks into 1-inch pieces and set aside.

Reduce the oven temperature to 350° F.

Soak the lasagna noodles in water to cover in a shallow dish until tender; sprinkle with the lemon juice and salt.

Melt the butter in a saucepan. Whisk in the flour. Cook over low heat until the mixture is smooth, whisking constantly. Add the chicken broth gradually. Cook until thickened, stirring constantly. Add the goat cheese. Heat until the goat cheese melts, stirring constantly.

Spread a thin layer of the cheese sauce in a rectangular baking dish. Layer 4 lasagna noodles in the bottom of the prepared dish. Layer half of the chopped asparagus stalks and half of the remaining cheese sauce over the lasagna noodles; sprinkle with some of the Parmesan cheese and pepper. Repeat layers with the remaining chopped asparagus stalks and cheese sauce. Top with the reserved asparagus tips and remaining Parmesan cheese.

Blend the garlic and herb cheese with the milk in a small bowl. Spread over the lasagna. Bake for 20 minutes or until bubbly.

Note This recipe should not be frozen.

SPINACH AND PORCINI LASAGNA

Serves Eight to Ten

Porcini, *the Italian word for a popular wild mushroom, actually means "piglet." In France the same mushroom is called cèpe. Dried porcini are available loose and in small packages.*

TO MAKE THE PORCINI BÉCHAMEL SAUCE:

Combine the dried mushrooms with the water in a small saucepan. Bring to a boil; remove from the heat. Let stand, covered, for 30 minutes. Drain, reserving about 1 cup of the liquid. Chop the mushrooms to measure about 1/2 cup.

Melt the butter in a small saucepan. Stir in the flour. Cook for 5 minutes, stirring constantly. Add the milk gradually, whisking constantly. Whisk in the reserved mushroom liquid. Cook over low heat for 8 minutes or until thickened, whisking constantly. Season with the salt and pepper.

TO MAKE THE LASAGNA:

Combine the spinach, ricotta cheese, eggs, 3 tablespoons of the Parmesan cheese, 1/4 cup of the parsley, nutmeg, and pepper in a bowl; mix well. Sauté the onion in the heated olive oil in a sauté pan for 5 minutes or until tender but not brown. Add the garlic. Sauté for 1 minute. Stir half the mixture into the spinach mixture.

Add the fresh mushrooms to the remaining onion mixture in the sauté pan. Sauté over medium heat for 10 minutes or until the mushrooms are tender and the liquid has evaporated. Add the chopped porcini, pepper, the remaining 1/4 cup parsley, and 2 tablespoons Parmesan cheese; mix well.

Preheat the oven to 350° F. Drain the lasagna noodles and pat dry. Arrange a layer of the noodles in a 10-by-14-inch baking dish. Spread with the spinach mixture. Arrange 1/3 of the mozzarella cheese slices randomly over the spinach mixture.

Add a second layer of noodles; spread the Light Red Sauce over the noodles. Top with half the remaining mozzarella cheese. Spread the mushroom mixture over the top and add the remaining mozzarella cheese. Top with the remaining noodles.

Spoon the porcini béchamel sauce over the top; sprinkle with the remaining 3 tablespoons Parmesan cheese.

Bake for 50 minutes or until the top is puffed and brown. Let stand for 15 minutes before serving.

For the porcini béchamel sauce

- 1 ounce dried porcini mushrooms
- 1 1/2 cups water
- 3 tablespoons unsalted butter
- 1/4 cup flour
- 1 cup milk
- salt and freshly ground pepper to taste

For the lasagna

- 2 10-ounce packages frozen chopped spinach, cooked
- 2 15-ounce containers ricotta cheese
- 2 eggs, beaten
- 8 tablespoons grated Parmesan cheese
- 1/2 cup chopped Italian flat-leaf parsley
- nutmeg and freshly ground pepper to taste
- 1 cup chopped onion
- 2 tablespoons olive oil
- 1 tablespoon chopped garlic
- 1 pound fresh mushrooms, sliced
- 1 pound lasagna noodles, cooked *al dente*
- 1 pound mozzarella cheese, thinly sliced
- 2 cups light red sauce (see page 166)

LIGHT RED SAUCE

A simple basic Italian sauce that always comes in handy.

1/2 cup chopped sweet yellow onion

1 tablespoon olive oil

1 clove of garlic, crushed

2 15-ounce cans Italian plum tomatoes

1 sprig of parsley

1 bay leaf

1/4 cup chopped fresh basil

1 teaspoon fresh oregano leaves

salt and freshly ground pepper to taste

Sauté the onion in the heated olive oil in a sauté pan over low heat for 5 minutes or until very tender but not brown. Add the garlic. Sauté for 1 minute.

Drain the tomatoes, reserving the juice in a bowl. Squeeze the remaining juice and seeds from the tomatoes into the bowl. Chop the tomatoes and add to the sauté pan. Strain the reserved juice into the sauté pan. Add the parsley and bay leaf.

Simmer the sauce for 10 minutes or until the sauce is reduced to 2 cups. Stir in the basil, oregano, salt, and pepper; discard the bay leaf.

Serve over pasta.

Note Look for tomatoes from the San Marzano Valley—truly Italy's best tomato.

PASTA CRUDA

Prepare this refreshing dish for a light summer luncheon on the patio.

1 1/2 pounds tomatoes, seeded

3 cloves of garlic, minced

1 cup chopped fresh basil

4 ounces mozzarella cheese, diced

1/2 cup extra-virgin olive oil

2 tablespoons balsamic vinegar

salt and freshly ground pepper to taste

1 pound uncooked pasta

Chop tomatoes. Combine the tomatoes, garlic, basil, cheese, olive oil, vinegar, salt, and pepper in a bowl; mix well. Let stand at room temperature for 1 to 6 hours.

Cook the pasta in a large pot of boiling water until *al dente*; drain. Add to the sauce; toss to mix well. Serve immediately.

Note For best results use a good quality fresh mozzarella cheese. To seed the tomatoes, cut into halves, and squeeze gently.

MANICOTTI WITH RATATOUILLE SAUCE

Serves Eight

T*he flavors of France and Italy are combined in the most pleasing way in this tasty dish.*

TO MAKE THE RATATOUILLE SAUCE:

Sauté the eggplant, onions, green pepper, and garlic in the olive oil in a sauté pan for 5 minutes.

Add the zucchini, oregano, basil, marjoram, salt, pepper, tomato sauce, and stewed tomatoes; mix well.

Simmer for 5 minutes or until the vegetables are tender.

TO PREPARE THE MANICOTTI:

Preheat the oven to 350° F.

Cook the manicotti using package directions; drain. Cool in a single layer on waxed paper.

Combine the cheeses, eggs, parsley, salt, and pepper in a bowl; mix well. Spoon into the manicotti.

Spoon half of the ratatouille sauce into a 9-by-13-inch baking dish. Arrange the filled manicotti in the prepared dish. Spoon the remaining sauce over the top.

Bake for 20 to 25 minutes or until bubbly.

For the ratatouille sauce

4 cups chopped peeled eggplant

2 cups sliced onions

2 cups green bell pepper strips

4 cloves of garlic, minced

6 tablespoons olive oil

4 cups sliced zucchini

1 teaspoon oregano

1 teaspoon basil

1/2 teaspoon marjoram
   salt and freshly ground pepper to taste

2 15-ounce cans tomato sauce

2 15-ounce cans stewed tomatoes

For the manicotti

8 ounces uncooked manicotti

32 ounces ricotta cheese

2 cups shredded mozzarella cheese

1/2 cup grated Parmesan cheese

2 eggs, slightly beaten

1/2 cup chopped parsley
   salt and freshly ground pepper to taste

PASTA NIÇOISE A LA GRECQUE

P*asta salad with a tangy twist.*

1½ pounds tuna steaks
4 tablespoons fresh lemon juice
1 tablespoon oregano
1 tablespoon rosemary
2 tablespoons capers
1 pound uncooked fusilli
2 tablespoons olive oil
1 3-ounce jar olive paste or tapenade, at room temperature
4–6 ounces whole pitted black olives, cut into halves lengthwise
6–8 ounces feta cheese
1 lemon, cut into wedges
parsley

Combine the fish with the lemon juice, oregano, rosemary, and capers in a shallow glass dish. Marinate, covered with plastic wrap, for 1 hour or longer.

Cook the pasta in a large pot of boiling water until *al dente*; drain and keep warm.

Microwave the tuna in the marinade on high for 4 to 5 minutes or until the fish flakes easily, rotating the dish after 2 minutes. Drain the tuna, reserving the marinade. Cut the tuna into bite-sized pieces. Strain the marinade, discarding the liquid and reserving the herbs and capers.

Combine the pasta with the olive oil in a serving bowl; toss to mix well. Add the olive paste, tuna, reserved herbs and capers, and half of the olives, tossing lightly. Spoon the pasta onto serving plates; sprinkle with some of the feta cheese. Garnish with the lemon wedges, remaining olives, and parsley. Serve with crusty bread and the remaining feta cheese.

Note The tuna may be grilled or broiled for 4 to 5 minutes or until done to taste and basted with the marinade.

Variation This dish could also be prepared with other meaty fish such as swordfish or shark, and other pasta, such as penne or rigatoni, could be substituted for the fusilli.

TOMATO AND SHRIMP LINGUINE

Serves Six

A *colorful addition to anyone's shrimp repetoire.*

Sauté the shrimp in 3 tablespoons of the olive oil in a sauté pan for 4 to 5 minutes or until the shrimp turn pink, stirring constantly. Remove the shrimp to a platter.

Sauté the mushrooms and garlic in the remaining 2 teaspoons of olive oil in the same sauté pan for 3 to 4 minutes or until the mushrooms are tender, stirring frequently. Add the tomatoes and lemon juice; mix well. Cook for 3 minutes, stirring frequently. Season with the salt, pepper, and crushed hot pepper.

Return the shrimp to the sauté pan; mix well. Cook just until heated through, stirring frequently.

Sprinkle with the cilantro or parsley. Serve with the linguine.

Variation For an Asian flair, use enoki mushrooms and serve with brown rice instead of linguine.

2 pounds medium shrimp, peeled, deveined

3 tablespoons plus 2 teaspoons virgin olive oil

1 pound large mushrooms, sliced

3 cloves of garlic, crushed

6 large plum tomatoes, chopped

3 tablespoons fresh lemon juice

salt and freshly ground pepper to taste

crushed hot pepper (optional)

2–3 tablespoons chopped fresh cilantro or parsley

1 pound cooked linguine

PASTA WITH SHRIMP AND SALMON

Serves Four

Serve this pasta at room temperature with crusty hot sourdough rolls and very cold Pinot Grigio wine for a winter supper, a summer picnic, or a fall tailgate party.

1 pound uncooked angel hair pasta

½ cup thinly sliced carrots

½ cup chopped red bell pepper

½ cup shelled fresh green peas

8 jumbo shrimp, cooked, peeled

8 ounces salmon fillet, poached

2 tablespoons capers

½ cup chopped plum tomatoes

1 pinch each of fresh basil, lemon pepper, crushed red pepper, and freshly ground black pepper

1 teaspoon salt

½ teaspoon herb pepper

2 tablespoons extra-virgin olive oil

wine vinegar to taste

grated Parmesan cheese to taste

Southern Italians first colonized Little Italy in the 19th century. In addition to popular restaurants, Little Italy now boasts of some of the tastiest bakeries.

Cook the pasta in a large pot of boiling water until *al dente*; drain. Steam the carrots, bell pepper, and peas until they are tender. Combine the pasta, steamed vegetables, cooked shrimp and salmon, capers, tomatoes, and seasonings in a large bowl. Add the olive oil and wine vinegar to taste; toss to mix well. Serve on individual plates; garnish with the Parmesan cheese.

Note This recipe may be made ahead but should not be frozen.

PASTA WITH RED PEPPER SAUCE

Serves Four

Capelli d'angelo, Italian for "angel hair," is a thin, delicate noodle that is best served in a very light sauce.

Sauté the bell peppers and carrots in the olive oil in a sauté pan for 4 to 5 minutes or until tender. Stir in the tomatoes, pear, garlic, basil, salt, and pepper. Simmer for 45 minutes.

Place the cooked pasta in a serving dish; spoon the sauce over the top. Serve with the Parmesan cheese.

Note For best flavor, use freshly grated Parmesan cheese, such as Parmigiano-Reggiano. Parmigiano-Reggiano's exceptional flavor and texture are the result of a longer aging process.

- 4 red bell peppers, chopped
- 2 carrots, finely chopped
- 1 tablespoon olive oil
- 2 cups canned tomatoes packed in purée
- 1/2 pear, chopped
- chopped garlic to taste
- 1 tablespoon fresh basil
- salt and freshly ground pepper to taste
- 1 pound uncooked angel hair pasta, cooked, drained
- grated Parmesan cheese to taste

RAVIOLI WITH WILD MUSHROOM SAUCE

Serves Eight

This rich ravioli recipe is from Jules Bistro in Manhattan's Greenwich Village.

Sauté the shallots, garlic, and mushrooms in heated olive oil in a saucepan until light brown. Add the chicken stock, cream, thyme, and rosemary. Simmer until of the desired consistency.

Cook the ravioli in a large pot of boiling water until tender; drain. Add to the sauce in the saucepan; mix gently.

Cook until heated through. Sprinkle with the parsley.

Note Ravioli will float to the top when cooked. Use oyster, shiitake, chanterelle, or other wild mushrooms.

- 2 cups chopped shallots
- 1/2 cup chopped garlic
- 16 ounces wild mushrooms
- 1 cup olive oil
- 3 cups chicken stock
- 3 cups heavy cream
- 1/4 cup chopped thyme leaves
- 1/4 cup chopped rosemary leaves
- 56 round ricotta cheese ravioli
- 1/2 cup chopped parsley

Paglia e Fieno with Salmon

Serves Four to Six

The fettucini in this dish is called *paglia e fieno*, which means, literally, *straw and hay* in Italian, and refers to the green and white colors of the pasta. It can also be made with all-spinach fettucini or with other kinds of fettucini.

12 ounces fresh spinach fettucini

12 ounces fresh egg fettucini

2 tablespoons olive oil

1 cup fresh or frozen small peas

   salt to taste

4 ounces smoked salmon, thinly sliced

1 pint heavy cream

1 tablespoon minced shallots

2 tablespoons white wine

   freshly ground pepper to taste

Cook the fettucini in a large pot of boiling water until *al dente*; drain. Toss with the olive oil in a bowl; set aside.

Cook the peas in boiling salted water to cover in a saucepan for 3 minutes; drain and refresh by rinsing in cold water. Set aside.

Purée 4 slices of the smoked salmon, 2 tablespoons cream, and shallots in a food processor until smooth. Cut the remaining smoked salmon into thin strips.

Bring the wine to a boil in a heavy saucepan. Add the remaining cream. Cook until the mixture coats the back of the spoon, stirring constantly. Stir in the salmon purée. Cook over low heat until heated through. Season with salt and pepper.

Combine the salmon sauce with the salmon strips, pasta, peas, salt, and pepper in a serving bowl; toss to mix well. Serve immediately.

PENNE IN VODKA SAUCE

This pasta dish seems to be turning up on virtually every menu in Manhattan. This version uses red pepper, giving the recipe an extra kick. Because the dish is so quick and easy, it is perfect to whip up at a moment's notice.

Melt the butter in a heavy saucepan. Add the olive oil, tomatoes, dill, red pepper flakes, and vodka. Cook over medium-high heat for 5 minutes; reduce the heat. Add the salt, sugar, and cream. Simmer until of the desired consistency.

Cook the penne in a large pot of boiling water until *al dente*; drain.

Combine the pasta with the sauce in a serving bowl; toss lightly to mix. Serve with the Parmesan cheese.

Note The vodka sauce may be made ahead and reheated, but do not boil.

Variation The red pepper flakes may be steeped in the vodka for 24 hours if desired. Vary the degree of spiciness with the amount of red pepper flakes.

4 ounces unsalted butter

1/2 cup olive oil

2 28-ounce cans whole peeled tomatoes, drained, chopped

1 teaspoon dill

1 teaspoon crushed red pepper flakes

1/4 cup vodka

1/4 teaspoon salt

1/4 teaspoon sugar

1 cup heavy cream

1 pound uncooked penne
grated Parmesan cheese
to taste

SESAME PASTA

Serves Four

Use tricolored corkscrew pasta or a garnish of lemon or orange sections to lend a colorful flair to this dish for special occasions.

For the dressing

5 tablespoons honey

1/2 cup sesame oil

5 tablespoons soy sauce

5 tablespoons white wine vinegar

1/4 cup toasted sesame seeds

For the pasta

10 ounces fresh spinach, chopped

3 scallions, finely chopped

8 ounces fresh mushrooms, sliced

1/4 cup unsalted butter

1 pound uncooked fresh tri-color pasta

1/2 cup minced fresh parsley

Left overleaf, travel just west of Little Italy and you will find yourself back in SoHo—another interesting downtown locale and the domain of fabulous cast-iron structures.

TO MAKE THE DRESSING:

Combine the honey, sesame oil, soy sauce, vinegar, and sesame seeds in a bowl; mix well and set aside.

TO PREPARE THE PASTA:

Sauté the spinach, scallions, and mushrooms in the butter in a sauté pan. Cool completely.

Cook the pasta in boiling water in a saucepan using package directions; drain well.

Combine the pasta with the sautéed vegetables and the dressing in a serving bowl. Add half the parsley; toss lightly. Chill until serving time. Garnish with the remaining parsley.

RIGATONI WITH PORCINI AND SAUSAGE
Serves Six

G*reat party fare. Can be prepared in advance, but take care to reheat gently.*

Soak the dried mushrooms in a bowl of hot water for 20 minutes; drain and reserve liquid.

Remove the sausage from the casing and crumble. Sauté in a sauté pan over low heat until the sausage is cooked through; drain and set aside.

Rinse the chicken and pat dry. Sauté in 1½ tablespoons of the butter in a sauté pan until the chicken is light brown.

Sauté the onion in the remaining 2½ tablespoons of butter in a large stockpot. Add the fresh mushrooms and drained porcini mushrooms. Sauté for about 5 minutes or until cooked through. Add the wine, beef stock, and herbs; mix well. Drain and reserve half the liquid. Add the sausage and the chicken; mix well. Stir in the cream. Simmer for 5 to 10 minutes or until the mixture is done to taste, adding some of the reserved liquid if more mushroom flavor is desired; discard the bay leaf.

Cook the pasta in a large pot of boiling water until *al dente*; drain. Combine with the sauce, Parmesan cheese, and pepper in a serving bowl; toss lightly to mix.

Note The sauce may be made ahead and also may be quadrupled and frozen for later use.

1 ounce dried porcini or
½ ounce dried porcini and
½ ounce dried morels

1 cup hot water

12 ounces sweet sausage

12 ounces boneless chicken, sliced

¼ cup unsalted butter

1 medium onion, chopped

1 pound fresh button and/or shiitake mushrooms, sliced

½ cup dry white wine

1 cup beef stock

1 teaspoon rosemary

1 bay leaf

1 cup heavy cream

1 pound uncooked rigatoni

1½ cups grated Parmesan cheese
freshly ground pepper to taste

VERMICELLI WITH ARTICHOKE HEARTS

This dish is as flavorful as it is colorful.

8 ounces vermicelli, cooked

1/2 cup large walnut pieces, toasted

1 cup green beans, cut into bite-sized pieces

2 6-ounce jars marinated artichoke hearts, drained, chopped

1 cup sliced fresh mushrooms

1/2 cup black olives

1 cup cherry tomatoes

1 red bell pepper, julienned

3 tablespoons chopped parsley

1/3 cup olive oil

1 clove of garlic, minced

1/2 teaspoon basil

1/4 teaspoon salt

freshly ground pepper to taste

From lemon bars and double-cream cheesecake to blackout cake, visitors and residents alike can indulge a craving for fine pastries.

Combine the vermicelli, walnuts, green beans, artichoke hearts, mushrooms, olives, tomatoes, bell pepper, and parsley in a large bowl.

Combine the olive oil, garlic, basil, salt, and pepper in a small bowl; mix well.

Pour over the pasta mixture; toss lightly to mix. Chill until serving time.

Variation Spaghetti or linguine may be substituted for vermicelli.

MINTED ORZO WITH CURRANTS

Serves Four

Serve this dish with baby lamb chops. It's a terrific update on the old mint jelly idea.

Cook the orzo in a small pot of boiling water for 5 minutes. Add the currants. Cook for 4 minutes longer or until the orzo is *al dente*; drain.

Combine the orzo mixture, butter, mint, parsley, and vinegar in a bowl; toss to mix well. Season with the salt and pepper to taste.

1 cup uncooked orzo

1/2 cup dried currants

2 tablespoons unsalted butter

1 tablespoon very finely chopped mint

1 tablespoon very finely chopped parsley

4 teaspoons white wine vinegar

salt to taste

freshly ground pepper to taste

The Alleva, in Little Italy, offers smoked mozzarella and homemade tiramisu, among other typically Italian specialities, to its customers.

WILD RICE AND CORN SALAD

Serves Ten to Twelve

This recipe is from Matt Delos, Head Chef at the Edson Hill Manor in Stowe, Vermont, and is an elegant accompaniment to any favorite poultry dish.

2 ears of corn, cooked

1 tablespoon finely chopped garlic

1/4 cup unsalted butter

1 tablespoon finely chopped onion

1 tablespoon finely chopped fresh thyme

2 cups wild rice

1 1/2 quarts chicken stock

1 bunch scallions, finely chopped

1 red bell pepper, finely diced

1 yellow bell pepper, finely diced

1 small red onion, finely chopped

salt and freshly ground pepper to taste

Cut the kernels from the corn; set aside.

Sauté the garlic in the butter in a sauté pan until tender, stirring constantly. Add the 1 tablespoon chopped onion and thyme; mix well. Stir in the wild rice and chicken stock. Bring the mixture to a boil; reduce heat. Simmer until the rice is tender.

Stir in the scallions, red pepper, yellow pepper, chopped red onion, corn, salt, and pepper. Cook just until heated through. The salad may be served at room temperature but is best when served warm.

Note For a summer presentation, grill corn in husks. Carefully remove husks from corn and reserve. When ready to serve, spoon salad into reserved husks.

JEWELED RICE SALAD

Serves Six to Eight

The name speaks for itself. The orange vinaigrette provides distinctive flavor and it looks just beautiful. A true gem of a dish.

TO MAKE THE DRESSING:

Combine the olive oil, orange juice, orange zest, lemon zest, salt, paprika, and cilantro in a bowl. Beat with a whisk until combined.

TO MAKE THE SALAD:

Thaw the peas in a colander under hot running water.

Combine the rice, peas, green olives, red pepper, and yellow pepper in a serving bowl; mix well. Add the dressing just before serving; toss gently. Serve from the bowl or on individual salad plates.

For the dressing

3 tablespoons olive oil

6 tablespoons orange juice

1 tablespoon grated orange zest

1 tablespoon grated lemon zest

1 teaspoon salt

1/2 teaspoon paprika

1/4 cup finely chopped fresh cilantro

For the salad

1 cup frozen peas

3 1/2 cups cooked white rice

2/3 cup sliced green olives

1/2 red bell pepper, chopped

1/2 yellow bell pepper, chopped

WILD MUSHROOM RISOTTO

Risotto is the classic rice specialty of northern Italy. This dish can either be served solo or as the sophisticated companion to a simple meat or fish dish.

Cook the peas in the water in a saucepan for 15 minutes or until tender; drain and set aside.

Sauté the mushrooms and 2 cloves of garlic in 3 tablespoons of the butter in a sauté pan for 3 to 5 minutes or until tender; set aside.

Sauté the shallots and 2 cloves of garlic in 3 tablespoons butter and olive oil in a saucepan until tender. Stir in the rice and wine. Cook until the wine is absorbed.

Increase the heat. Add ½ cup of the chicken stock every 5 minutes. Cook until the liquid is absorbed between additions. Add the peas with the remaining ½ cup chicken stock. Cook until the rice is tender but firm and creamy; remove from the heat.

Add the mushrooms, Parmesan cheese, salt, and pepper; toss lightly to mix. Serve immediately.

Note This risotto may be served as a side dish or, with a salad, as the main dish for a vegetarian dinner.

At left, on Lafayette Street, a sculpture store sells molds to make plaster architectural elements, such as those used on the Main Post Office at Eighth Avenue and 33rd Street.

1 cup freshly shelled peas

1 cup water or chicken broth

8 ounces shiitake mushrooms

8 ounces cremini mushrooms

4 cloves of garlic, minced

6 tablespoons unsalted butter

3–4 shallots, minced

3 tablespoons virgin olive oil

2 cups uncooked Arborio rice

½ cup dry white wine

5½ cups hot chicken stock

4 ounces grated Parmesan cheese

salt and freshly ground pepper to taste

MOREL AND ASPARAGUS RISOTTO

Serves Six

Morels are delicious in season, but this dish may be made just as easily with other mushrooms. Arborio is the rice of choice for risotto.

15 medium stalks asparagus

6 ounces bacon, chopped

2 medium onions, chopped

12 ounces fresh morels

1/4 cup unsalted butter

1 1/2 cups uncooked Arborio rice

3–4 cups hot chicken stock

2/3 cup grated Parmesan cheese

salt and freshly ground pepper to taste

Peel the asparagus stems and cut the stalks into 1-inch pieces. Parboil the asparagus in boiling water in a saucepan; drain.

Cook the bacon in a saucepan until light brown. Add the onions. Sauté over low heat until the onions are tender.

Cook the morels in the butter in a sauté pan until tender. Add the morels to the onion mixture. Stir in the rice. Add the hot chicken stock gradually, stirring constantly. Cook until the rice is tender, stirring frequently; the mixture will be creamy and thick. Stir in the asparagus, Parmesan cheese, salt, and pepper; toss lightly. Serve immediately.

NUTTED WILD RICE SALAD

Serves Eight

Bring this salad to a summer picnic or the opera in Central Park as a 1990's update to potato salad and coleslaw.

8 ounces wild rice

1 cup pecan halves

1 cup golden raisins

1/2 cup fresh orange juice

grated zest of 1 large orange

4 scallions, sliced

1/4 cup olive oil

1 1/2 teaspoons salt

Cook the wild rice using the package directions. Drain if necessary. Cool to room temperature.

Combine the wild rice, pecans, raisins, orange juice, orange zest, scallions, olive oil, salt, and pepper in a bowl; mix well. Season with additional salt if needed.

Note The flavor is enhanced by preparing this salad in advance.

Variation Substitute dried cranberries for all or part of the raisins to add color.

PARK PICNIC CHEESE-HERB BREAD

Serves Six to Eight

Whether picnicking in the shadow of Belvedere Castle while waiting to see **A Midsummer Night's Dream** or meeting friends for a concert on the Great Lawn, this bread will enhance a memorable evening.

Preheat the oven to 375° F.

Dissolve the sugar in the lukewarm water in a bowl; mix well. Stir in the yeast. Let stand in a warm place for 15 minutes.

Sift the flour, salt, dry mustard, and pepper into a bowl; mix well. Stir in the chives, parsley, and 1½ cups cheese. Add the yeast mixture, stirring until a soft dough forms.

Knead the dough on a lightly floured surface for 10 minutes. Place in a buttered bowl.

Let rise, covered with plastic wrap, in a warm place for 1 hour or until doubled in bulk. Knead on a lightly floured surface for 5 minutes.

Shape the dough into a loaf. Place in a buttered 5-by-9-inch loaf pan. Let rise, covered with plastic wrap, for 40 to 50 minutes or until doubled in bulk.

Sprinkle with the remaining ½ cup cheese. Bake for 40 to 45 minutes or until golden brown. Remove to a wire rack to cool completely.

Note This bread should not be frozen.

1 teaspoon sugar
1¼ cups lukewarm water
1 envelope dry yeast
3 cups unbleached flour
2 teaspoons salt
1 teaspoon dry mustard
¼ teaspoon freshly ground pepper
2 teaspoons chopped fresh chives
2 tablespoons chopped fresh parsley
2 cups finely shredded cheddar cheese

KNICKERBOCKER BEER BREAD

Serves Eight

A perfect companion to a hearty stew or thick soup. Preparation only takes a minute. The oven does the rest.

Preheat the oven to 350° F.

Combine the flour, sugar, and beer in a bowl; mix well.

Spoon into a greased 5-by-9-inch loaf pan.

Bake for 50 minutes.

3 cups self-rising flour
3 tablespoons sugar
1 12-ounce bottle of beer

ENDINGS

CAKES

COOKIES

PIES AND TARTS

Even good things must come to an end ... thank goodness for the delectable endings found on the following pages. They are, to an ingredient, irresistible. Every good chef knows that a fabulous finale is the way to leave a lasting impression on dinner guests. As the final jewel in the crown of your dinner party, your dessert should dazzle. Whether fruits and nuts are your passion, chocolate your temptation, or silky smooth custard your heart's desire, you will find them all in this chapter of happy endings.

A light and refreshing Light Apricot Soufflé with Red Currant Raspberry Coulis may provide the perfect ending, or a rich and creamy Crème Brulée with Cherries may be the right final flavor. Offer a sinful Chocolate Soufflé Cake to guests who confess a weakness for chocolate, or present a luscious Fig and Berry Clafouti for a classic close. The choice will not be easy but is guaranteed to please.

When the final aria has been sung at the Opera, the final curtain has fallen on Broadway, the last dance has been played at the Ball—when no one wants to go home—this is the time to host a *Midnight Dessert Buffet*. The setting of choice may be the elegant and classic National Academy of Design, where many famous artists received their training. The Academy's graceful Fifth Avenue location is spacious yet intimate—the perfect place to enjoy the sensational selection of desserts offered in this chapter's sample menu. These are desserts with a true New York flair and range from an Empire Cheesecake to TriBeCa Truffles. The rich and sophisticated tastes of Pears à la Vigneronne and Chocolate Pâté are balanced by the simple yet spectacular flavors of Chocolate Spice Cookies and Butter Pecan Crescents. These delectable confections are sure to bring a smile of delight and pleasure to your thankful guests.

Cakes and cookies, pies and tarts, puddings and soufflés, shortbreads and biscotti—all are found in this bittersweet chapter of happy endings. Dessert is an ending to look forward to, like the bitter cold days of a New York winter or the stifling heat of a Manhattan summer. End as you begin—with a celebration of tastes, flavors, and textures that define gracious entertaining.

MENU
Midnight Dessert Buffet

PENTHOUSE TRUFFLE CAKE

EMPIRE CHEESECAKE

PEARS A LA VIGNERONNE

CHOCOLATE SPICE COOKIES

BUTTER PECAN CRESCENTS

TRIBECA TRUFFLES

CHOCOLATE PATE

HAZELNUT BISCOTTI

CHAMPAGNE AND
SPARKLING WATER

ESPRESSO BAR

Left overleaf, *Diana, a larger-than-life bronze,*
holds court at Manhattan's
National Academy of Design.

Far left above, *Pears à la Vigneronne on Red Currant Raspberry Coulis.*

Near left above, *a guest's selection of delectable sweets.*

Left below, *Chocolate Pâté with chocolate-dipped leaves,*
Hazelnut Biscotti, and a centerpiece of fresh fruits with sugar-frosted grapes.

Above, *Empire Cheesecake, a bounty of fresh strawberries,*
Penthouse Truffle Cake, and tiered finger confections.

Right overleaf, *TriBeCa Truffles, Butter Pecan Crescents,*
and Chocolate Spice Cookies
elegantly presented on a tiered silver compote.

LIGHT APRICOT SOUFFLE

Serves Four

This elegant dessert doubles easily and is low in fat.

Preheat the oven to 350° F. Butter a 1½-quart soufflé dish. Sprinkle lightly with sugar.

Beat the egg whites in a bowl until stiff peaks form but the egg whites are not dry. Add the brown sugar. Beat just until blended. Fold in the apricot purée gently. Stir in the salt and vanilla.

Spoon the mixture into the prepared soufflé dish. Sprinkle with sugar. Place the dish in a shallow pan of hot water. Bake for 30 minutes. Serve with Red Currant Raspberry Coulis (this page) if desired.

Note To make the apricot purée, plunge apricots into boiling water for 2 minutes. Drain, then cover with cool water to loosen skins. Half and pit the apricots. Put the apricots back into a saucepan with a small amount of water. Cook over low heat until soft (about 5 minutes). Purée in a food processor.

sugar to taste

5 egg whites

5 tablespoons sifted brown sugar or granulated brown sugar

¾ cup apricot purée, about 12 apricots

salt to taste

½ teaspoon vanilla extract

red currant raspberry coulis (optional)

RED CURRANT RASPBERRY COULIS

Serves Eight to Ten

A fine topping for ice cream or for frozen yogurt for the cholesterol-conscious as well as an exquisite accent to the Light Apricot Soufflé, Lemon Soufflé, or Pears à la Vigneronne.

Bring the jelly and the undrained raspberries to a boil in a saucepan, stirring occasionally. Reduce the heat. Stir in the cornstarch, salt, and sugar. Cook over low heat for 20 to 30 minutes or until the sauce is clear and thickened, stirring constantly.

Strain the sauce. Allow it to cool. Chill, covered, in the refrigerator.

Variation May use two 10-ounce boxes of frozen raspberries instead of fresh raspberries, and ½ cup sugar.

1 cup red currant jelly

2 pints fresh raspberries

1 teaspoon cornstarch

salt to taste

1 cup sugar

FROZEN AMARETTO SOUFFLE

Chocoholics will enjoy this treat topped off with a hot fudge sauce.

For the almond macaroons

1 cup blanched almonds
1 cup sugar
1 teaspoon vanilla extract
2 egg whites
confectioners' sugar

For the soufflé

5 egg yolks
3 eggs
½ cup superfine sugar
⅓ cup amaretto
1 cup finely crushed almond macaroons
2 cups heavy cream, whipped

TO MAKE THE ALMOND MACAROONS:

Preheat the oven to 350° F.

Grind the almonds with the sugar in a food processor.

Combine the vanilla and egg whites in a bowl; mix well. Add the almond mixture; mix well. Shape the mixture into 12 balls.

Place the balls on a parchment-lined cookie sheet; flatten the balls slightly. Brush with water; sprinkle with the confectioners' sugar.

Bake in the top third of the oven for 15 to 18 minutes or until light brown. Slide the parchment onto a moist towel; let stand just until the parchment is moist. Remove the macaroons immediately.

TO MAKE THE SOUFFLE:

Prepare a 5-cup soufflé dish with a foil collar extended 2 inches above the rim of the dish.

Combine the egg yolks, eggs, and sugar in a bowl. Beat at a high speed for 10 to 12 minutes or until light and very thick. Add the amaretto and almond macaroons. Beat at a low speed until combined.

Fold in the whipped cream gently until no white streaks remain. Spoon into the prepared soufflé dish. Freeze overnight.

Remove the collar gently from the soufflé. Roll the edge carefully in additional macaroon crumbs if desired.

LEMON SOUFFLE

Serves Four to Six

This traditional soufflé can be served alone or with Red Currant Raspberry Coulis.

Preheat the oven to 375° F. Butter a 2-quart soufflé dish; dust with the confectioners' sugar.

Beat the egg yolks in a bowl until very light. Add the sugar. Beat for 5 minutes or until the sugar dissolves and mixture is creamy. Add the lemon juice and lemon zest, beating until combined.

Beat the egg whites in a bowl until stiff peaks form. Fold in the egg yolk mixture gradually. Spoon the mixture into the prepared soufflé dish. Place in a pan of water. Place foil around the dish to form a collar. Bake for 35 minutes.

confectioners' sugar for dusting
7 egg yolks
1/2 cup sugar
1/2 cup fresh lemon juice
zest of 2 lemons
7 egg whites

CHOCOLATE PATE

Serves Eight to Twelve

A true chocolate-lover's delight, this sumptuous dessert melts in your mouth.

Melt the bittersweet chocolate and butter with the cream in a double boiler over low heat, stirring occasionally to blend well. Remove from the heat.

Whisk in the egg yolks 1 at a time. Whisk in the confectioners' sugar and rum gradually. Spoon the mixture into a 4-cup loaf pan lined with plastic wrap. Let stand at room temperature until cool. Chill, covered, overnight.

Invert the pâté onto a platter; remove the plastic wrap. Chill until serving time. Cut with a cold knife or wire cutter to serve.

Note This chocolate pâté is a "make-ahead" indulgence.

16 ounces best-quality bittersweet chocolate, broken up
1/4 cup unsalted butter
1 cup heavy cream
4 egg yolks
1 cup sifted confectioners' sugar
1/2 cup dark rum

FIG AND BERRY CLAFOUTI

Serves Six

A *marriage of figs and berries makes this country-French dessert extra special.*

1 pound fresh figs

1/2 cup fresh raspberries, blueberries, or blackberries

1/4 cup whole blanched almonds

2 tablespoons flour

3/4 cup milk

1/3 cup plus 2 tablespoons sugar

2 eggs

1 tablespoon port or Marsala

1/4 teaspoon salt

2 tablespoons chilled unsalted butter, sliced

Preheat the oven to 400° F.

Cut the figs into halves lengthwise. Arrange the figs cut side up in a buttered 5-cup gratin dish. Sprinkle the berries into the dish.

Grind the almonds with the flour in a food processor until very fine. Combine the mixture with the milk, 1/3 cup sugar, eggs, wine, and salt in a medium mixer bowl; mix well.

Pour the batter into the prepared dish. Dot with the butter; sprinkle with the 2 tablespoons sugar. Bake for 30 to 40 minutes or until the top is golden brown and the mixture is set. Serve warm or at room temperature. Garnish with a fresh mint sprig.

HASTY PUDDING

Serves Fifteen to Twenty

C *hef Arnold Fanger of the Harvard Club has reduced the Club's famous Hasty Pudding recipe to proportions manageable for most kitchens.*

1 1/4 cups sugar

1 tablespoon ginger

1 1/2 teaspoons cinnamon

1/2 teaspoon nutmeg

1/2 gallon milk

1/4 cup unsalted butter

2 cups molasses

1 1/4 cups Quaker cornmeal

salt to taste

Mix the sugar with the ginger, cinnamon, and nutmeg in a small bowl. Combine the sugar mixture with the milk, butter, and molasses in a saucepan.

Bring the mixture to a boil. Stir in the cornmeal and salt. Cook for 10 to 15 minutes or until thickened, stirring constantly. Serve the pudding warm with a scoop of vanilla ice cream.

At right, the Metropolitan Life Insurance Company added a 700-foot tower in 1909 to its original building, erected in 1893. The illuminated tower served as the company's symbol of "the light that never fails."

CITY CREME BRULEE WITH CHERRIES

Serves Six

The addition of cherries brings this classic crème brûlée to new heights.

12 ounces Bing cherries, pitted
2/3 cup water
1/2 cup superfine sugar
2 teaspoons arrowroot
2 teaspoons ice water
2 tablespoons Kirsch
5 egg yolks
   vanilla extract to taste
2 1/4 cups heavy cream, scalded

Combine the cherries, water, and 1/4 cup sugar in a saucepan. Cook over medium heat until the sugar dissolves, stirring constantly. Simmer for 3 minutes, stirring occasionally. Stir in a mixture of the arrowroot and ice water. Simmer for 2 minutes, stirring occasionally. Add the Kirsch; mix well. Spoon the mixture into 6 ramekins.

Combine the eggs yolks and vanilla in a small bowl; mix well. Stir a small amount of the cream into the egg yolk mixture; stir the egg yolk mixture into the cream. Strain the mixture into a saucepan.

Cook over low heat for 10 minutes or until thickened, stirring constantly. Do not boil. Cover with waxed paper; cool. Spoon the mixture into the prepared ramekins. Chill for 3 hours.

Sprinkle with the remaining 1/4 cup sugar. Place the ramekins on a baking sheet. Broil for 7 minutes. Allow to cool before serving. Garnish with additional Bing cherries.

TIRAMISU

Serves Four

From the restaurant Josephina, this recipe is lower in fat and cholesterol.

2 ounces espresso
1/2 ounce Kahlua
1/2 ounce Tia Maria
4 ounces maple syrup
16 ladyfingers
8 ounces mascarpone cheese
8 ounces nonfat sour cream
4 egg whites, stiffly beaten

Combine the espresso, liqueurs, and 1 ounce of maple syrup in a bowl; mix well. Add the ladyfingers; let soak for 5 seconds. Arrange the ladyfingers over the bottom and sides of an 8-by-8-inch dish.

Combine the cheese, sour cream, and 3 ounces of the maple syrup in a bowl; mix well. Fold in the egg whites with a wooden spoon.

Spoon the cheese mixture over the ladyfingers. Chill, covered with plastic wrap, overnight. Garnish with a sifting of baking cocoa.

BIG APPLE CRISP

Serves Ten

An autumn delight that pleases all palates.

Preheat the oven to 350° F.

Arrange the apple slices in a greased 9-by-13-inch baking dish.

Sift the sugar, flour, salt, and spices into a bowl. Blend in butter. Press the mixture over the apples. Drizzle with the butter.

Bake for 35 to 40 minutes or until brown.

Serve either hot or cold with whipped cream or vanilla ice cream.

5–6 apples, sliced
1 cup sugar
1 cup flour
salt to taste
$1\frac{1}{2}$ teaspoons cinnamon
1/2 teaspoon nutmeg
$\frac{1}{2}$ teaspoon allspice
$\frac{1}{2}$ cup melted unsalted butter

NECTARINES WITH SPICED CARAMEL

Serves Two

A union of summer's bounty and fall flavors.

Melt the butter in a small sauté pan over low heat. Add the brown sugar, cinnamon, ginger, allspice, Grand Marnier, and lemon juice; mix well. Add the nectarines. Boil for 30 seconds, stirring constantly.

Serve in stemmed goblets with Hazelnut Biscotti.

Variation May substitute pears, oranges, apples, peaches, or strawberries for the nectarines.

3 tablespoons unsalted butter
3 tablespoons dark brown sugar
$\frac{1}{4}$ teaspoon cinnamon
$\frac{1}{4}$ teaspoon ginger
$\frac{1}{8}$ teaspoon allspice
3 tablespoons Grand Marnier
2 tablespoons fresh lemon juice
2 nectarines, sliced

METROPOLITAN PEACHES

Serves Six

A *perfect ending to a summer evening. Serve with whipped cream and a glass of chilled amaretto.*

6 firm ripe peaches

1/2 cup sugar

1/2 cup sliced blanched almonds

6 large amaretto cookies or almond macaroons, broken into pieces

1 egg yolk

1/4 cup amaretto

Preheat the oven to 350° F.

Cut the peaches into halves; remove the pits. Scoop 1 tablespoon peach pulp from each half. Place the peach halves in a buttered baking dish.

Combine the peach pulp, sugar, almonds, cookie pieces, egg yolk, and liqueur in a food processor. Process until smooth. Spoon the peach mixture evenly into the peach halves.

Bake for 20 to 25 minutes or until heated through. Serve warm or at room temperature.

PEARS A LA VIGNERONNE

Serves Six

B *eautiful served on Red Currant Raspberry Coulis.*

8 ripe fresh pears

2 cups dry white wine

1/2 cup sugar

zest of 1 lemon

1/4 teaspoon cinnamon

1 teaspoon vanilla extract

1/4 cup orange marmalade

1/2 cup apricot preserves

Left overleaf, musicians practicing at Carnegie Hall, located on West 57th Street.

Peel and core whole pears; do not remove stems.

Bring the pears, wine, sugar, and lemon zest to a boil in a stockpot, stirring occasionally. Add water to cover the pears as necessary. Reduce the heat. Simmer for 5 to 10 minutes or until the pears are tender, stirring gently.

Transfer the pears and lemon zest to a serving bowl.

Bring the liquid in the stockpot to a boil. Stir in the cinnamon, vanilla, orange marmalade, and apricot preserves. Cook for 10 minutes, stirring gently.

Spoon the sauce and lemon zest over the pears. Cool to room temperature. Chill until serving time.

LUSCIOUS BLACKBERRY CAKE

Serves Eight

U*se a bountiful berry harvest to make this family favorite.*

Preheat the oven to 350° F.

Beat the egg whites in a bowl until foamy. Add ¼ cup sugar 1 tablespoon at a time, beating until stiff peaks form.

Cream the butter and ¾ cup sugar in a bowl until light and fluffy. Add the salt and vanilla; mix well. Beat in the egg yolks until creamy.

Add a mixture of 1½ cups flour and baking powder alternately with the milk, mixing well after each addition.

Coat the blackberries with 1 tablespoon flour. Fold the blackberries into the batter. Fold in the meringue gently.

Spoon the batter into a buttered and floured 8-by-8-inch cake pan. Sprinkle with the 1 tablespoon sugar.

Bake for 50 minutes or until the cake tests done.

Variation May substitute blueberries for blackberries.

2 egg whites

1 cup plus 1 tablespoon sugar

½ cup unsalted butter or margarine, softened

¼ teaspoon salt

1 teaspoon vanilla extract

2 egg yolks

1½ cups plus 1 tablespoon flour

1 teaspoon baking powder

⅓ cup milk

1½ cups fresh or frozen blackberries

CRANBERRY JEWEL CAKE

Wonderful and tart—a single layer of cake covered with sparkling cranberries. A brush of red currant jelly on the cranberries after baking makes them glisten.

3/4 cup unsalted butter, softened

1 cup sugar

6 cups fresh cranberries

1 1/4 cups sifted flour

1 1/2 teaspoons baking powder

1/4 teaspoon salt

1 large egg

1 teaspoon vanilla extract

2/3 cup milk

1/3 cup red currant jelly

Preheat the oven to 350° F.

Spread half of the butter over the bottom and sides of a 9-inch cake pan. Sprinkle with half of the sugar. Spread the cranberries in the prepared pan.

Sift the flour, baking powder, salt, and remaining sugar together.

Cream the remaining butter in a bowl until smooth. Beat in the egg and vanilla. Add the dry ingredients 1/3 at a time, alternating with the milk and mixing just until moistened after each addition. Mixture may appear slightly curdled.

Pour the batter carefully over the cranberries. Place the pan in the bottom third of the oven. Bake for 1 hour. Cool the cake on a wire rack for 20 minutes. Loosen the sides with a knife and invert the cake onto a serving plate.

Melt the jelly in a heavy saucepan over medium heat. Cool slightly. Spoon evenly over the cranberries. Serve the cake at room temperature with vanilla ice cream or sweetened whipped cream.

CHOCOLATE SOUFFLE CAKE

Serves Eight to Ten

This cake looks beautiful when topped with confectioners' sugar sprinkled through a stencil.

TO MAKE THE CAKE:

Preheat the oven to 275° F. Butter and flour a 10-inch round cake pan and line with a circle of parchment paper.

Combine the chocolate, butter, orange zest, vanilla, and almonds in a double boiler. Cook over hot water until the chocolate and butter melt, stirring occasionally. Cool to lukewarm.

Beat the egg yolks with half the sugar in a bowl until thick and lemon-colored. Fold in the chocolate mixture gently with a rubber spatula.

Beat the egg whites in a bowl until foamy. Add the remaining sugar gradually, beating until stiff peaks form. Blend lightly into the chocolate batter with a spatula.

Spoon the batter into the prepared pan. Bake for 1 hour and 20 minutes. Loosen the cake from the side of the pan with a knife. Invert the cake onto a wire rack and again onto a second wire rack so that the cake is right side up. The cake will have a crisp sugar crust and will sink slightly. Let stand until cool.

Sprinkle the cake with confectioners' sugar and cut into wedges to serve. Serve with the crème anglaise.

TO MAKE THE CREME ANGLAISE:

Beat the egg yolks and sugar in a mixer bowl until thick and lemon-colored.

Blend the cornstarch with a small amount of the cold milk. Add to the remaining milk in a saucepan; mix well. Scald the milk, stirring constantly. Add to the egg yolk mixture gradually, whisking constantly. Pour the mixture into a heavy pan, preferably of tin-lined copper; do not use an aluminum pan.

Cook the custard over low to medium heat to 164° F. on a candy thermometer, or until the mixture starts to coat a wooden spoon, stirring constantly; do not cook over too high heat or the eggs will curdle.

Strain the custard into a clean, dry bowl. Stir in the vanilla. Cool to room temperature, stirring occasionally to prevent a skin from forming. If desired, chill, covered with plastic wrap, in the refrigerator.

For the cake

7 ounces semisweet chocolate, chopped

7 tablespoons unsalted butter

grated zest of 1 orange

2 teaspoons vanilla extract

1 tablespoon finely ground almonds

5 egg yolks

9 tablespoons sugar

5 egg whites

sifted confectioners' sugar

For the crème anglaise

8 egg yolks

1/2 cup sugar

1 teaspoon cornstarch

4 cups milk

1 teaspoon vanilla extract

WALNUT SOUR CREAM CAKE

V*ery moist and great for breakfast too.*

½ cup unsalted butter, softened

1½ cups sugar

2 eggs, beaten

1 cup sour cream

1 teaspoon baking soda

1½ cups flour

1½ teaspoons baking powder

1 teaspoon vanilla extract

½ cup chopped walnuts

1 teaspoon cinnamon

Preheat the oven to 350° F.

Cream the butter and 1 cup sugar in a bowl until light and fluffy. Add the eggs; mix well.

Stir in a mixture of the sour cream and baking soda. Add a mixture of the flour and baking powder; mix well. Stir in the vanilla. Fold in the walnuts.

Spoon the batter into a greased 8-by-8-inch cake pan. Bake for 30 to 40 minutes or until the cake tests done. Combine the remaining ½ cup sugar and cinnamon in a bowl; mix well. Sprinkle over the cake while still warm.

Note This cake freezes well.

PENTHOUSE TRUFFLE CAKE

T*he top of this elegantly rich cake may be decorated with confectioners' sugar, sifted over the top through a doily or cut-out stencil. Serve with whipped cream or a raspberry or strawberry sauce.*

8 ounces amaretto cookies, crushed

¼–½ cup Grand Marnier or Kirsch

16 ounces dark chocolate

½ cup unsalted butter, softened

2 egg yolks

2½ cups heavy cream, whipped

confectioners' sugar

Soak the crushed cookies in the liqueur in a bowl.

Melt the chocolate in a double boiler over hot water. Remove from the heat. Stir in the butter. Stir a small amount of the chocolate mixture into the egg yolks; stir the egg yolks into the chocolate mixture; mix well. Let stand to cool.

Fold the whipped cream into the chocolate mixture.

Alternate layers of the chocolate mixture and the cookies in a greased 8-inch springform pan until all the ingredients are used. Chill for several hours before serving.

Decorate the top with confectioners' sugar.

Serves Ten to Twelve

A wonderful lemon-marsala crust with true New York-style filling. Garnish with a variety of berries, from red currants to raspberries, blackberries, or champagne grapes to add a contrast both in color and taste.

TO MAKE THE PASTRY:

Cut the butter into the flour in a bowl until crumbly; make a well in the center. Combine the egg yolks, 3 tablespoons sugar, lemon zest, and wine in a bowl; beat with a fork until smooth. Pour into the well in the crumb mixture; mix well to form a pastry. Knead until smooth.

Line the bottom and side of a 9-inch springform pan with the pastry. Chill in the refrigerator.

TO MAKE THE FILLING:

Preheat the oven to 325° F.

Cream the 1⅓ cups sugar and the cream cheese in a bowl until light and fluffy. Add the 1 cup sour cream, ricotta cheese, and 1 teaspoon vanilla; mix well. Add the eggs one at a time, beating well after each addition.

Spoon the cream cheese mixture into the prepared pan. Place the pan in the center of the lower or middle rack of the oven. Bake for 50 minutes or until set. Cool the cheesecake on a wire rack.

TO MAKE THE TOPPING:

Chill the sour cream, ½ teaspoon vanilla, and 2 tablespoons sugar in a bowl. Beat until creamy. Spread the mixture almost to the edge of the cooled cheesecake.

Preheat the oven to 350° F. Bake the cheesecake for 5 minutes or turn off the oven and place the cheesecake in the cooling oven for 50 minutes.

Variation Graham cracker crumbs or a pound cake mix may be substituted for the pastry. Prepare a pound cake mix using package directions. Spoon one-fourth of the pound cake batter into the bottom of the springform pan.

For the pastry

½ cup unsalted butter
1½ cups sifted flour
2 egg yolks
3 tablespoons sugar
1 teaspoon grated lemon zest
1 tablespoon dry Marsala

For the filling

1⅓ cups sugar
16 ounces cream cheese, softened
1 cup sour cream
15 ounces ricotta cheese
1 teaspoon vanilla extract
4 eggs

For the topping

1 cup sour cream
½ teaspoon vanilla extract
2 tablespoons sugar

LINZER HEART COOKIES

Yields Eighteen Cookies

Serve these festive cookies on Valentine's Day, or any time you are looking for an extra-special sweet.

3 ounces cream cheese, softened

½ cup unsalted butter, softened

1¼ cups sifted flour

¼ teaspoon salt

2 tablespoons milk

1 cup raspberry preserves

confectioners' sugar

Beat the cream cheese and butter in a bowl until light and fluffy. Add the flour and salt; mix well. Stir in the milk. Shape the dough into a ball. Chill in the refrigerator for 1 hour or longer.

Preheat the oven to 450° F.

Roll the dough ¼ inch thick on a floured surface. Cut the dough into heart shapes with a cookie cutter. Place the cookies on a greased cookie sheet. Cut a circle out of half the cookies with a 1-inch cookie cutter.

Bake for 8 to 10 minutes or until light brown. Remove to a wire rack to cool. Spread each solid heart with 2 teaspoons preserves. Place hearts with holes on top of the prepared cookies. Sprinkle with the confectioners' sugar.

BUTTER PECAN CRESCENTS

Yields Thirty-Six Crescents

Easy enough for every day yet pretty enough for the holidays.

1 cup unsalted butter, softened

2 cups flour

1 cup sugar

1 teaspoon vanilla extract

1 cup broken pecans

confectioners' sugar

Cream the butter in a blender. Add the flour, sugar, vanilla, and pecans. Process until combined.

Shape the dough into 2-inch crescents or rolls. Place the crescents on an ungreased cookie sheet.

Place the cookies in a cold oven. Do not preheat the oven. Bake at 350° F. for 25 to 30 minutes or until light brown. Remove to a wire rack to cool.

Roll the cookies in the confectioners' sugar.

Note To form the crescents, roll dough between your palms into a ½-inch thick rope. Cut into 2-inch long pieces and shape into crescents.

BUTTER COOKIE SHORTBREADS

Yields Forty-Eight Cookies

Who would guess that these yummy cookies owe some of their flavor to potato chips?

Preheat the oven to 325° F.

Cream the butter and sugar in a bowl until light and fluffy. Add the flour, beating until smooth. Stir in the vanilla and crushed potato chips.

Drop by teaspoonfuls onto an ungreased cookie sheet. Bake for 10 to 15 minutes or until the cookies are light brown. Remove the cookies to a wire rack to cool completely.

Variation For an extra treat, dip the cooled cookies into melted chocolate.

- 1 cup unsalted butter, softened
- 3/4 cup sugar
- 1 1/2 cups flour
- 1 teaspoon vanilla extract
- 3/4 cup finely crushed potato chips

IRISH CREAM COOKIES

Yields Forty Cookies

An Irish secret makes these chocolate chip cookies the best ever.

Preheat the oven to 375° F.

Cream the butter, sugar, and brown sugar in a bowl until light and fluffy. Add the egg and vanilla; mix well. Add the Irish Cream; mix well.

Beat a mixture of the flour, baking soda, and salt into the creamed mixture. Fold in the pecans and chocolate chips.

Drop by teaspoonfuls onto an ungreased cookie sheet. Bake for 8 to 10 minutes or until light brown. Remove to a wire rack to cool.

- 1/2 cup unsalted butter, softened
- 1/2 cup sugar
- 1/2 cup packed brown sugar
- 1 egg
- 1 teaspoon vanilla extract
- 1/4 cup Bailey's Irish Cream
- 2 1/4 cups flour
- 1/2 teaspoon baking soda
- 1/2 teaspoon salt
- 3/4 cup chopped pecans
- 1 cup semisweet chocolate chips

HOLIDAY FRUIT COOKIES

P*recious cookies packed with flavor. They are wonderful for holiday gift-giving.*

1 7-ounce can sweetened condensed milk

2 cups chopped walnuts

2 cups chopped dates

2 cups shredded coconut

2 teaspoons vanilla extract

Preheat the oven to 350° F.

Combine the condensed milk, walnuts, dates, coconut, and vanilla in a bowl; mix well.

Roll the mixture into small balls. Place on a greased cookie sheet.

Bake for 10 minutes or until light brown. Remove the cookies to a wire rack to cool.

TRIBECA TRUFFLES

T*he downtown denizens of TriBeCa, or the "triangle below Canal Street," are known for their au courant urban chic. These truffles, served with champagne, add a sophisticated touch to any menu.*

8 ounces best quality semisweet chocolate, broken

1/4 cup Grand Marnier

2 tablespoons strong brewed coffee

1/2 cup unsalted butter, cut into 1-inch pieces

6 ounces gingersnaps, finely crushed

1 tablespoon vanilla extract

1/2 cup confectioners' sugar

Combine the chocolate with the liqueur and coffee in a small saucepan; cover. Place the saucepan in a larger pan of boiling water; remove from the heat. Let stand for 5 minutes or until melted.

Beat in the butter 1 piece at a time with a portable mixer. Add the cookie crumbs and vanilla; mix well. Chill for several hours.

Shape the chocolate mixture into balls. Roll in confectioners' sugar; place in bonbon cups.

Chill until serving time. Store in the refrigerator or freezer for up to several weeks.

Variation Substitute Kahlua for the Grand Marnier and crushed chocolate wafers for the gingersnaps. Roll in 1/2 cup baking cocoa instead of the confectioners' sugar.

CHOCOLATE SPICE COOKIES

Yields Forty-Eight Cookies

These cookies can double as holiday cookies. They make exceptional ginger boys!

Preheat the oven to 350° F.

Cream the butter and sugar in a bowl until light and fluffy. Beat in the eggs. Sift the flour, baking cocoa, cinnamon, ginger, cloves, and salt together. Add to the creamed mixture; beat until smooth.

Shape the dough into a flattened ball. Chill for 1 hour or longer. Roll the dough ⅛ inch thick on a floured surface. Cut into the desired shapes.

Bake the cookies on an ungreased cookie sheet for 8 to 10 minutes. Remove to a wire rack to cool.

1½ cups unsalted butter, softened
1¾ cups sugar
2 large eggs, slightly beaten
3 cups sifted flour
1½ cups baking cocoa
1 teaspoon cinnamon
2 teaspoons ground ginger
½ teaspoon ground cloves
¼ teaspoon salt

WALL STREET KISSES

Yields Thirty-Six Kisses

Bulls and bears alike will delight!

Preheat the oven to 375° F.

Cream the butter, confectioners' sugar, and vanilla in a bowl until light and fluffy. Add the flour and walnuts. Beat at a low speed until combined.

Shape a small amount of the dough around each chocolate kiss, forming a sphere. Place on an ungreased cookie sheet. Bake for 12 minutes or until the cookies are set but not brown. Roll the warm cookies in additional confectioners' sugar. Cool on a wire rack.

1 cup unsalted butter, softened
½ cup confectioners' sugar
1 teaspoon vanilla extract
2 cups sifted flour
1 cup finely chopped walnuts
1 6-ounce package milk chocolate kisses
confectioners' sugar for dusting

HAZELNUT BISCOTTI

Yields Twenty-Four Biscotti

These traditional Italian biscuits are perfect for dipping into dessert wine or coffee.

1 cup hazelnuts, lightly toasted, skinned, coarsely chopped

1 cup sugar

1/2 cup melted unsalted butter

1/4 cup hazelnut liqueur or brandy

3 eggs

3 cups flour

2 teaspoons baking powder

1/4 teaspoon salt

Preheat the oven to 350° F.

Combine the hazelnuts, sugar, butter, liqueur, and eggs in a bowl; beat until smooth. Stir in the flour, baking powder, and salt. Knead the mixture briefly; shape into a roll 2 inches in diameter. Place on a nonstick or parchment-lined cookie sheet.

Bake the roll for 25 minutes or until firm; the roll will have a cakelike texture. Cool on a wire rack.

Slice the roll diagonally into 1/2-inch slices; place the slices on a cookie sheet. Bake for 20 minutes, turning once to brown both the sides evenly. Cool the cookies to room temperature. Store in an airtight container. Serve with coffee.

MAPLE CHOCOLATE PRALINES

Yields Fifty Pralines

A marriage made in heaven for chocolate lovers: a Georgian pecan plantation and the Vermont maple woods get together to create a sensation of their own.

Bring the confectioners' sugar, maple syrup, cream, and chocolate to a boil in a double boiler, stirring constantly until blended.

Cook, covered, for 2 minutes or until the steam washes the sugar crystals from side of the pan. Cook, uncovered, to 234° F. on a candy thermometer, the soft-ball stage. Do not stir. Remove from the heat. Allow to cool to 110° F. on a candy thermometer.

Beat with a wooden spoon until the mixture begins to thicken and becomes opaque. Stir in the pecans. Drop by tablespoonfuls onto waxed paper. Let stand until firm. Store the pralines in an airtight container.

2 cups confectioners' sugar
1 cup pure maple syrup
1/2 cup heavy cream
2 ounces bittersweet chocolate
2 cups pecans, broken into large pieces

Previous page, the Waldorf-Astoria Hotel, an Art Deco classic, was designed by Schultz & Weaver in 1931. It has hosted every United States president since Herbert Hoover, as well as innumerable celebrities and foreign dignitaries.

At left, the former headquarters of American Telephone and Telegraph, located at 195 Broadway, was a triumph of design by Welles Bosworth. Its facade boasted more columns than any other building in the world. Tall arched windows yielded panoramic views of lower Manhattan for the winged **Golden Boy,** *now regilded and relocated to the new AT&T building at Madison Avenue and 56th Street.*

MADISON SQUARES

Moist, chewy brownies full of macadamias!

3/4 cup flour

1/4 teaspoon baking powder

1/4 teaspoon salt

1 cup sugar

2 eggs

1/3 cup melted unsalted butter

1/3 cup baking cocoa

1 teaspoon vanilla extract

3/4 cup coarsely chopped
    macadamia nuts

Preheat the oven to 350° F. Butter the bottom and sides of an 8-by-8-inch baking pan.

Mix the flour, baking powder, and salt in a small bowl.

Combine the sugar, eggs, and butter in a bowl; mix well. Stir in the baking cocoa and vanilla.

Add the flour mixture to the egg mixture; mix well. Stir in the macadamia nuts.

Spread in the prepared baking pan. Bake for 30 to 35 minutes or until the brownies test done.

Cool on a wire rack. Cut into squares.

Variation For Brownie Petits Fours, cut cooled brownies, using a hot, wet knife, into 1-inch squares. Melt 8 ounces semisweet chocolate in a double boiler over medium heat. Cool slightly. With a fork, carefully dip each brownie square into the chocolate, coating evenly. Drain on wire rack. Garnish with candied violets or nuts, white chocolate, or even baby rosebuds.

APPLE LINGONBERRY CRUMB PIE

Serves Eight

S*candinavian and American classics meet, creating a scrumptious cold weather dessert. Especially good served with vanilla ice cream.*

Preheat the oven to 350° F.

Combine the apples with a mixture of 10 tablespoons brown sugar, cinnamon, cornstarch, and lemon juice in a bowl; mix well. Spread evenly in the pie shell. Sprinkle the lingonberries over the top.

Combine the 1 cup brown sugar, butter, and flour in a bowl, stirring until crumbly. Spread the crumb mixture over the lingonberries. Bake for 30 to 40 minutes or until brown. Serve warm or cold with vanilla ice cream.

6 Granny Smith apples, peeled, sliced

10 tablespoons (about 2/3 cup) plus 1 cup packed dark brown sugar

1 tablespoon cinnamon

2 teaspoons cornstarch

2 tablespoons fresh lemon juice

1 baked 9-inch pie shell

3 ounces Swedish lingonberries or raspberries

1 cup unsalted butter, softened

2 cups flour

DRIPPING SPRINGS PECAN PIE

Serves Six

A *decadent dessert that will please pecan pie lovers and chocolate lovers alike.*

Preheat the oven to 450° F.

Combine the eggs, molasses, corn syrup, brown sugar, vanilla, salt, and melted butter in a bowl; mix well. Stir in the pecans and chocolate chunks.

Spoon the mixture into the pie shell. Bake for 10 minutes. Reduce the oven temperature to 325° F. Bake for 45 minutes or until the center of the pie is set. Cool on a wire rack. Serve warm or at room temperature.

Variation Drizzle extra melted chocolate over the top of the pie. Allow the pie to cool and the chocolate to harden.

3 eggs, beaten

2 tablespoons molasses

3/4 cup dark corn syrup

1 cup packed dark brown sugar

1 teaspoon vanilla extract

1/8 teaspoon salt

1/4 cup melted unsalted butter

1 1/3 cups pecan halves

3/4 cup chocolate chunks

1 unbaked 9-inch pie shell

LEMON TART

This Lemon Tart has been on the menu of Café Luxembourg since it opened in 1983.

For the almond crust

2 cups all-purpose flour

1/4 cup almond flour

2 tablespoons sugar

1/4 cup confectioners' sugar

1/2 teaspoon salt

3/4 cup unsalted butter, chilled, chopped

1/4 teaspoon almond extract

1/4 teaspoon vanilla extract

1 egg

For the lemon curd

4 eggs

1 cup sugar

1/2 cup lemon juice

1 cup unsalted butter

For the garnishes

whipped cream or crème fraîche

sprigs of mint

TO MAKE THE ALMOND CRUST:

Combine the all-purpose flour, almond flour, sugar, confectioners' sugar, and salt in a bowl. Add the butter; mix until crumbly. Add the flavorings and egg; mix lightly to form a dough.

Shape the dough into a flattened ball. Chill in the refrigerator. Preheat the oven to 350° F.

Roll the dough on a floured surface. Fit into a fluted 10-inch tart pan with a removable bottom; prick the bottom with a fork. Bake for 15 to 20 minutes or until golden brown. Cool to room temperature.

TO MAKE THE LEMON CURD:

Combine the eggs, sugar, lemon juice, and butter in a saucepan; mix well. Cook over medium heat just until the mixture begins to bubble and thicken, whisking constantly.

Strain the curd immediately into the tart shell. Chill the tart in the refrigerator until set.

TO SERVE THE TART:

Remove the side of the tart pan. Place the tart on a serving plate. Top each serving with whipped cream or crème fraîche and garnish with a sprig of mint.

Variation To make lemon curd tartlets as shown on page 114, prepare above recipe substituting miniature tartlet pans for the 10-inch tart pan. Cooking time will be reduced (depending on the size of tartlet pans). Bake until golden brown. Garnish with fresh blackberries, raspberries, currants, or strawberries.

RESTAURANTS

*We would like to thank
the following restaurants
and caterers in Manhattan
for providing recipes in
I'll Taste Manhattan:*

ARCADIA

AUREOLE

BOULEY

CAFE DES ARTISTES

CAFE LUXEMBOURG

DANIEL

DE MARCO

ERMINIA

THE FOUR SEASONS

THE HARVARD CLUB

IL CANTINORI

JOSEPHINA RESTAURANT

JULES BISTRO

LE CIRQUE

LES TROIS PETITS COCHONS

NEUMAN & BOGDONOFF

NEW YORK JUNIOR LEAGUE HEADQUARTERS

THE PARTY BOX

ROSA MEXICANO

THE RUSSIAN TEA ROOM

THE STANHOPE HOTEL

TAVERN ON THE GREEN

Elizabeth Smith Alpert ◆ Janice L. Ambruso ◆ Hope Kent Annan ◆ Lisa Arnold ◆ Renee Babenzien ◆ Sarah Bachman ◆ Claudia Backlund ◆ Dawn Balogh ◆ Patricia Read Barry ◆ Sam Bassman ◆ Barbara Batcheler ◆ Jill A. Bayer ◆ Grace Beacham ◆ Emily G. Becnel ◆ Amy Beim ◆ Joan M. Benham ◆ Mrs. F. Henry Berlin ◆ Linda Newman Bernstein ◆ Melissa Lewis Bernstein ◆ Patricia A. Bevis ◆ Marilyn Blumberg ◆ Gloria Veeder Bond ◆ Stephanie E. K. Borynack ◆ Jeanne Boutelle ◆ Patricia Bowden ◆ Beverly Bradley ◆ Caroline F. Brady ◆ Jennie Brown ◆ Diana Buchanan ◆ Noreen Buckfire ◆ Hayley M. Budd ◆ Jo Buford ◆ Kim Burmester ◆ Stephanie Busby ◆ Barbara Callahan ◆ Kara Cambell ◆ Elizabeth M. Camougis ◆ Kathryn L. Campbell ◆ Jeanne A. Campbell ◆ Julie Cappos ◆ Liz Cappos ◆ Christina Carney ◆ Lea Carroll ◆ Mrs. Arch Wilson Cassidy ◆ Ann R. Cathcart ◆ Elizabeth G. Caulo ◆ Rosemary Citrano ◆ Virginia Citrano ◆ Marjorie Blythe Cobb ◆ Sandy Codd ◆ Pam Conte ◆ Jeannie Lawson Conway ◆ Danica Cordell-Reeh ◆ Edith Coulson ◆ Thelma White Cousins ◆ Susan U. Crafford ◆ Alicia Crawford ◆ Louise Weir Creel ◆ Ellen Cromack ◆ Mary Dallenbach ◆ Norah Daly ◆ Laura Danforth ◆ Mary Daniel ◆ Jennifer Daugherty ◆ Evie Davis ◆ Paulette Deglas ◆ Marilyn deLeo ◆ Joan Dempsey ◆ Maureen Denn ◆ Anne Dewey ◆ Susan Doherty ◆ Liz Ann Doherty ◆ Elizabeth Heard Donald ◆ Cydney Donnell ◆ Susan Douglas ◆ Elizabeth P. Draper ◆ Bernice Blythe Dunn ◆ Maureen Dunn ◆ Cynthia B. English ◆ Mrs. Alanson T. Enos ◆ Vicky Evangelidis ◆ Peyton Evans ◆ Ann Ewell ◆ Rosalie Feaser ◆ Christina M. Feicht ◆ Mary Ferguson ◆ Ann Finaly ◆ Ellen Finkelstein ◆ Francis M. Fisher ◆ Betty Fisk ◆ Mary Flournoy ◆ Jennifer Foley ◆ Alison Foster ◆ Diana Worth Foster ◆ Amy Fraim ◆ Jean Frame ◆ Dian Friedman ◆ Frank Fuchs ◆ Peter Fuchs ◆ Richard J. Fuchs ◆ Gloria Fulton ◆ Susan Garcia ◆ Alyce Garver ◆ Irvine Allen Gaskin ◆ Bill Geist ◆ Jody Geist ◆ Michelle Gerwin ◆ Karen Gillespie ◆ Patricia E. Glendon ◆ Sue-Gray Goller ◆ Margaret L. Goodman ◆ Katie Gottshall ◆ John Gottshall ◆ Helen E. Graham ◆ Marjorie Greer ◆ Katharine Greity ◆ Thomas C. Hack ◆ Megan H. Hagerty ◆ Cindy Hale ◆ Maret Halinen ◆ Courtenay Hardy ◆ Rhoda Harris ◆ Jeannine Harris ◆ Dorinda Scharff Hawkins ◆ Emma Hayes ◆ Barbara Shook Hazen ◆ Mary Grace Heine ◆ Pamela B. Hendrickson ◆ Ellen Heydet ◆ Carol Humstone ◆ Joyce Hutchins ◆ Elizabeth Illium ◆ Libby Jacobson ◆ Margaret Johnson ◆ Whitney Jones ◆ Cynthia Keiser ◆ Allison Cooke Kellogg ◆ Mary Kelly ◆ Melissa A. Kelly ◆ Joyce Kenyon ◆ Mrs. Fredd Kidder ◆ Eugenia King ◆ Sherry Kossick ◆ Jane Kovel ◆ Ellen Kratzer ◆ Pam Krauss ◆ Lisa Lacher-Bryan ◆ Kevin Lally ◆ Mary-Lou Leddy ◆ Dorothy Leonard ◆ Diane Leventhall ◆ Margaret S. Lewis ◆ Roger Lewis, Jr. ◆ Vi Lilly ◆ Mrs. Michael R. Linburn ◆ Eugenia Ling ◆ Jean Veeder Logan ◆ Marian MacKinney Lorch ◆ Jane A. Lyons ◆ John M. Manacella ◆ W. Richmond Marshall III ◆ Mary McCaffery ◆ Tom McCaffery ◆ Holli McCuistion ◆ Mary McDonald ◆ Suzanne McGee ◆ Jean McGrail-Kefeli ◆ Julia McGrath ◆ Julie McLaughlin ◆ Janet A. McMillan ◆ Susan Menelaides ◆ Vernon L. Merrill ◆ Bernard Mignot ◆ Mikael Moller ◆ Judy Tamm Morton ◆ Jessica Murphey ◆ Susan Nagel ◆ Madeleine P. Naylor ◆ Betsy Newell ◆ Ruthann G. Niosi ◆ Zoila E. Noguerole ◆ Dorothea E. Nolan ◆ Kara Orr ◆ Sarah Hewitt Owens ◆ Brett Paben ◆ Barbara Paddock ◆ Cynthia B. Palicka ◆ Bettie B. Pardee ◆ Ellissa Parnon ◆ Susan Van Pelt ◆ Anne Page Pendarvis ◆ Allyson Perre ◆ Eleanor Peterkin ◆ Connie Peters ◆ Joe Pignatelli ◆ Nan Pollack ◆ Julia Porter ◆ Devon Postiglione ◆ Julie Prall ◆ Sheri Ptashek ◆ Elise M. Quasebarth ◆ Christine M. Rafalko ◆ Michelle Randall ◆ Erin Randall-Orgel ◆ Cynthia S. Richards ◆ Joanna J. Richardson ◆ Mary Alice Rickert ◆ Deirdre Riou ◆ Patrice Rodden ◆ Diann Rohde ◆ Deborah Romaine ◆ Francis A. Root ◆ Alison Roscoe ◆ Lynne R. Roth ◆ Francene Rugendorf ◆ Mary Ruth ◆ Gina Ryan ◆ Linda Saage ◆ Elizabeth Standish Sackson ◆ Mark A. Sanok ◆ Donna Sardisco ◆ Julie T. Sargent ◆ Jennie Scaife ◆ Angel Schade ◆ Lara Elizabeth Schmidt ◆ Susan Schreiber ◆ Donna Senko ◆ Mary Ann Shickich ◆ Elizabeth Schaupp Sidles ◆ Katharine Sigety ◆ Thomas Sikorski ◆ Christian Sippel ◆ Maureen Skillman ◆ Grady Smith ◆ Laura Smith ◆ Sally Ann Sockwell ◆ Mary C. Soloman ◆ Leslee Sherrill Spoor ◆ Mrs. Stafiniak ◆ Laura Passantino Stegman ◆ Lucy P. C. Steinert ◆ Arden Stephenson ◆ Carolina Sterling ◆ Varina H. Stuart ◆ Sarah Steves ◆ Elizabeth Stewart ◆ Jayne Sutton ◆ Mary-Powel Thomas ◆ Anne Bahr Thompson ◆ Trish Tidwell ◆ Anthony Tinervia ◆ Tom Tobin ◆ Ginny Tortolani ◆ Blanche Trauger ◆ Ann R. Trotter ◆ Arlene Tynan ◆ Mrs. Senen Ubina ◆ Renee T. Vasey ◆ Stacy Waggoner ◆ Alexis Walker ◆ Sarah C. Walters ◆ Sally M. Ward ◆ Jeannette S. Warner ◆ Vickie Bostock Waters ◆ Edye Tarbox-Weill ◆ Susan Wetchler Weill ◆ Nancy Wekselbaum ◆ Melissa Welsh ◆ Nicholas White ◆ Missy White ◆ Mary G. Whitley ◆ Christina C. Wilde ◆ Wendy Willett ◆ Eileen Willner ◆ Ellen Willner ◆ Lane Wilson ◆ Heather Wilson ◆ Betty Winters ◆ Stacy Womsley ◆ Shere Yellin ◆ Mary Youngling

DESIGN SOURCES

All addresses, except where noted, are in Manhattan. Items not identified and not credited are privately owned.

FRONT JACKET
Evening Supper

Porcelain plates—Solanée,
866 Lexington Avenue;
Tablecloth—Léron Inc., 750
Madison Avenue.

Cocktails in a SoHo Loft

pages 17-20, private loft apartment
in SoHo.

Lunch Under Sail

Pages 53-56, The Yacht Petrel.
Available for private charter out of
Battery Park, 212-825-1976.
Page 53, food storage
containers—Gracious Homes,
1220 Third Avenue.
Page 54, crystal champagne
cooler—Tiffany & Company,
727 Fifth Avenue.
Page 55, antique nautical quilt—
Laura Fisher Antique Quilts and
Coverlets, 1050 Second Avenue;
wood and brass-handled serving tray
and serving implements—Keesal &
Matthews, 1244 Madison Avenue;
sterling silver mint julep cups—
Tiffany & Company, 727 Fifth
Avenue; antique teak deck chair and
antique silver flatware—Jules Bistro,
96 St. Marks Place.

A Restaurant Sampler

Page 73, sterling silver champagne
cooler—Tiffany & Company, 727

Fifth Avenue; Comte D'Artois
Ancienne Manufacture Royale
porcelain—Bernardaud-Limoges,
777 Madison Avenue; bed and table
linens—Léron Inc., 750 Madison
Avenue.

A Holiday Celebration

Pages 93-96, the New York Junior
League Headquarters.
Page 93, garlands and
wreaths—Brownstone Studios,
685 Third Avenue; Powerscourt
Waterford crystal goblets—
The Waterford Wedgewood Store,
713 Madison Avenue; Chinese
Bouquet Rust Herend porcelain
salad plate—Scully and Scully,
504 Park Avenue; Singapour
porcelain serving plate—
Bernardaud-Limoges,
777 Madison Avenue.
Page 95, Chinese Bouquet
Rust Herend porcelain soup
tureen and platter—Scully and
Scully, 504 Park Avenue;
Singapour porcelain serving
plates—Bernardaud-Limoges,
777 Madison Avenue.
Page 96, Christmas tree and
decorations—Brownstone Studios,
685 Third Avenue.

Tea in the Garden

Page 113, assorted hats—Tracey
Tooker, 18 Mercer Street.
Page 114, Rothschild Bird
Herend porcelain plates—Scully and
Scully, 504 Park Avenue;

antique silver flatware—Jules
Bistro, 96 St. Marks Place
Page 115, bowl and spoon—
Keesal & Matthews,
1244 Madison Avenue;
floral arrangement—Larkspur,
39 Eighth Avenue

Picnic in the Park

Page 133, antique quilt—Laura
Fisher Antique Quilts and Coverlets,
1050 Second Avenue.

Pasta Kitchen Party

Pages 153-156, private apartment
on Fifth Avenue.

Midnight Dessert Buffet

Pages 189-192, the
National Academy of Design,
1089 Fifth Avenue.
Gold fabric cloth and red
tassels—Clarence House, 111
Eighth Avenue; assorted large tea
trays, 3-tier pastry server, serpentine
table—The Posh Party, Party
Rentals, 868 Kent Avenue,
Brooklyn; silver oblong tray, green
lacquer footed cake stand and silver
champagne cooler—Christofle
Pavilion,
680 Madison Avenue; Jaguar Jungle
Lynn Chase Designs dessert
plate—Scully and Scully, 504 Park
Avenue; beverages—Acker Merrall
and Condit, 160 West 72nd Street.

PHOTOGRAPH INDEX

NORTH OR HUDSON

EAST OR SOUND

NEW YORK